International Trade in Services

International Trade in Services

Effective Practice and Policy

Sarita D. Jackson

A PRODUCTIVITY PRESS BOOK

First published 2021 by
Routledge
600 Broken Sound Parkway #300, Boca Raton FL, 33487

and by Routledge
2 Park Square, Milton Park, Abingdon, Oxon, OX14 4RN
Routledge is an imprint of the Taylor & Francis Group, an informa business

© 2021 Taylor & Francis

ISBN: 9780367463304 (hbk)
ISBN: 9780367462642 (pbk)
ISBN: 9781003028208 (ebk)

Typeset in Garamond
by Deanta Global Publishing Services, Chennai, India

Contents

SECTION II GUIDE TO EXPORTING A SERVICE

Preface

What about the services sector? That single question that I raised at an international trade panel discussion in 2014 sparked my interest and the need to write this book.

Months earlier, I moved from the Southeast region of the United States back to my hometown, Los Angeles, to start my own international trade market research company. This move followed years spent in the private sector and academia. The panel discussion included mostly government officials who shared with the audience facts and figures about exporting to the global market. The examples given focused on trade in goods. This is understandable considering that the Port of Los Angeles is the busiest port in the United States.

However, services, such as logistics and transportation, play a role in moving cargo from one port to another. Nevertheless, the conversation did not touch on the role of many services in the area of international trade. Hence, the question: What about the services sector? As a researcher myself, I asked about any data on local service providers who are exporting overseas, as well as the opportunities and challenges that they encounter. The response, simply put, was that the information did not exist.

Not long after that panel discussion, I became involved in offering training sessions, workshops, and courses on international trade. As I looked for material on international trade in services for the business audience, much of what I found were scholarly texts and highly technical publications on this topic. A couple of times, a participant asked me about texts on exporting a service or workshops solely focused on the services sector.

From these observations and experiences, I write this book to offer an easy-to-understand and thorough guide on international trade in services from both the business and policy levels.

Acknowledgments

The development of the idea for this book began not long after I started my own international trade research firm in 2013. However, the book itself would not have come to fruition without the support and assistance from a number of people throughout the writing process. There are key individuals whose efforts and contributions must be acknowledged.

I am grateful to Yohan Nah for his keen insight and contributions based on his understanding of trade agreements, digital trade, and foreign direct investment. The information that he shared and his review of one of the chapters proved invaluable. Furthermore, Thaise Dias met with me virtually on a regular basis while based in Brazil to share any updates on Brazilian laws as they related to the book's subject matter. Daniel Frachou's contribution of any additional data that could be inserted into the book helped to advance the research process, as well.

The government officials and business owners who responded immediately and took time out of their schedules for an interview and to share additional insight cannot be thanked enough. Those individuals include Anthony Andrews, Norman Arikawa, Veronica Contreras, Hema Dey, Andrea Ewart, Jim Gitney, Devorah Kaufman, Maurice Kogon, and Mac Maison.

Finally, the tireless efforts of my immediate family members—Dorothy Jackson (mother), Nathaniel Jackson (father), and Kevin Jackson (brother)—to provide the space, resources, and encouragement became invaluable, especially toward the end of the process.

Dorothy Jackson's readings and feedback on each chapter based on her global business experience kept me encouraged to keep writing and to remember my purpose for the book. Such encouragement was definitely needed, as the majority of the writing process occurred during a year filled with many unexpected, life-altering events.

The personal time that Kevin Jackson volunteered also contributed to the completion of this project. Some of his unforgettable contributions include, but are not limited to, helping to transcribe interviews and add information to different software programs, even when we would end up working late into the night or starting early in the morning.

The listening ear and words of wisdom that Nathaniel Jackson has always given me throughout each journey that I have embarked on throughout my life, once again, helped me to stay focused and keep moving forward.

Thanks goes to my family and those close friends who showed their genuine support, understanding, and patience.

About the Author

Sarita D. Jackson, PhD, is the founder, president, and CEO of the Global Research Institute of International Trade (GRIIT), a U.S.-based think-tank and consulting firm. Her firm helps companies to increase their revenues through competitive exports via up-to-date, data-driven, customized market research and strategy development.

Dr. Jackson is also an author, TEDx speaker, and business school instructor. She received her B.A. degree in broadcast journalism and Spanish from the University of Southern California and earned her PhD in political science (emphasis on comparative and international political economy) from Brown University.

Acronyms

ACP	African, Caribbean, and Pacific
ADB	Asian Development Bank
AFCFTA	African Continental Free Trade Area
AFDB	African Development Bank
AGOA	African Growth and Opportunities Act
AI	Artificial Intelligence
APS	Annual Program Statement
ASEAN	Association of Southeast Asian Nations
BAA	Broad Agency Announcement
BIT	Bilateral Investment Treaty
CAFTA-DR	Dominican Republic-Central American Free Trade Agreement
CBP	Customs and Border Protection
CBI	Caribbean Basin Initiative
CBTPA	Caribbean Basin Trade Preferences Act
CDB	Caribbean Development Bank
CENPROMYPE	Regional Center for the Promotion of Micro-Small-and-Medium Enterprises
CITD	Centers for International Trade Development
CPC	Central Product Classification
CPI	Co-production International
CPTPP	Comprehensive and Progressive Agreement for Trans-Pacific Partnership
CSME	Caribbean Single Market Economy
DFID	UK Department for International Development
DOS	Department of State
DSB	Dispute Settlement Body
DUNS	Data Universal Numbering System

ECCB	Eastern Caribbean Central Bank
ECLAC	Economic Commission for Latin America and the Caribbean
EFTA	European Free Trade Association
EIN	Employer Identification Number
EOI	Expression of Interest
ESM	Emergency Safeguard Measure
ETAP	Export Trade Assistance Program
EU	European Union
EY	Ernst and Young
FDI	Foreign Direct Investment
FedEx	Federal Express
GATS	General Agreement on Trade and Services
GATT	General Agreement on Tariffs and Trade
GDP	Gross Domestic Product
GNI	Gross National Income
GSP	Generalized System of Preferences
IBRD	International Bank for Reconstruction and Development
ICC	International Chamber of Commerce
IDB	Inter-American Development Bank
IDFC	International Development Finance Corporation
INBIA	International Business Innovation Association
IFI	International Financial Institutions
IGBA	Illegal Gambling Business Act
IISD	International Institute for Sustainable Development
IoT	Internet of Things
IT	Information Technology
ITA	International Trade Association
ITO	International Trade Organization
MDB	Multilateral Development Bank
MENA	Middle East and North Africa
Mercosur	Southern Common Market
MFN	Most Favoured Nation
MNC	Multinational Company
MCC	Millennium Challenge Corporation
NAFTA	North America Free Trade Agreement
NEI	National Export Initiative
NFO	Notice of Funding Opportunity
OECD	Organization for Economic Cooperation and Development

OFII	Organization for International Investment
OPIC	Overseas Private Investment Corporation
PESTLE	Political, Economic, Sociocultural, Technological, Legal, Environmental
PPA	Protocol of Provisional Application
RFP	Request for Proposal
RTA	Reciprocal Trade Agreement
SACU	Southern African Customs Union
SAM	System for Award Management
SBA	Small Business Administration
SEO	Search Engine Optimization
SIDS	Small Island Developing States
SME	Small-and-Medium-Sized Enterprise
STEP	State Trade Expansion Program
SW	Single Window
SWE	Single Window Environment
SWOT	Strengths-Weaknesses-Opportunities-Threats
TIDCA	Trade, Investment, and Development Cooperative Agreement
TIFA	Trade and Investment Framework Agreement
TIN	Taxpayer Identification Number
TiSA	Trade in Services Agreement
TFA	Trade Facilitation Agreement
TOR	Terms of Reference
TPP	Trans-Pacific Partnership
TRIPS	Trade Related Aspects of Intellectual Property Rights
UK	United Kingdom
UKTPO	UK Trade Policy Observatory
UNCTAD	United Nations Conference on Trade and Development
UNDB	United Nations Development Business
UNDP	United Nations Development Programme
UNEP	United Nations Environment Programme
UNESCO	United Nations Educational, Scientific, and Cultural Organization
UPS	United Parcel Service
US	United States
USAID	U.S. Agency for International Development
USCBC	US-China Business Council
USDA	U.S. Department of Agriculture

USITC	U.S. International Trade Commission
USMCA	United States-Mexico-Canada Agreement
USTR	U.S. Trade Representative
WGI	Worldwide Governance Indicator
WCO	World Customs Organization
WTO	World Trade Organization

Chapter 1

Bringing Services Trade to the Discussion

Ten students, many of whom run small businesses in the manufacturing and agricultural sectors, sat in the first session of an 11-week course on international trade being taught online. The online version was a change from the normal experience of anywhere from between 15 and 40 students from all around the world sitting in one classroom at a university in the city of Los Angeles. Although the clock on the computer read 6:30 p.m. Pacific Time, the international trade course was being taught to students sitting in their homes in different time zones and regions, which included Asia and the Middle East. The shift from classroom to virtual instruction resulted from the physical distancing measures put in place in response to the 2020 global health pandemic. In this case, an educational service transcended physical borders and reached individuals abroad through the use of digital technology and a small camera.

The unexpected shifts in daily routine, behavior, interests, etc., caused by a global health pandemic demonstrated the significant role that the services sector plays in the global economy. Furthermore, the increased dependence on specific types of services has exacerbated the need for two things: 1) an in-depth and practical discussion on the global market opportunities for service suppliers and 2) a guide on how to leverage the different opportunities that exist.

Oftentimes service was left out of the discussions on international trade because of the fact that it is an intangible commodity. For example, economists ignored trade in services because they did not think that services were tradable, as World Bank economists Bernard Hoekman and Carlos A. Primo Braga discuss in their 1997 paper "Protection and Trade in Services." As this book shows, that has not been the case, even in an historical context.

Practical policy discussions about the impact of international trade on domestic firms, workers, and consumers, at least in the United States, have tended to focus mostly on the manufacturing sector. In 2016, the U.S. trade deficit was the focus of the U.S. presidential campaign. The trade deficit reached a little over US$500 billion, per statistics collected from the International Trade Centre. What did not dominate the airwaves and social media was that the trade deficit was the result of greater imports of goods than exports. In goods alone, the 2016 trade deficit figure was much higher at almost US$800 billion. At the same time, the United States had a trade surplus just under US$300 billion in service, which contributed to a lower overall trade deficit.

The minimal focus on services trade and its contribution to overall trade balance spills over into the practices designed to help businesses to compete globally. International trade educational efforts organized by state and local government agencies for the business community for example, predominantly emphasize trade in goods. As a result, discussions about opportunities, policies, and resources are tailored to an audience of manufacturers and agricultural producers. Unfortunately, the audience members who are in the services sector receive minimal, if any, information on selling a service to consumers in a foreign market.

This book speaks to that audience. Furthermore, the book is designed to serve as a single, comprehensive guide for service suppliers trying to navigate the international trade arena. To add value to the information provided, interviews were conducted with several small business owners and a representative of a global market research firm. These interviews focused on the opportunities and challenges that the interviewees and/or their clients have faced when providing a service overseas. Finally, the interviews are used as case studies to highlight key lessons for services exporters that align with the appropriate chapter.

Each chapter offers a simple and thorough discussion about international trade in services. The first section of the book looks at the history of trade in services, the trends in international trade in services, and the patterns of foreign direct investment in the services sector. The following section takes the reader on a step-by-step journey of identifying market opportunities, selecting the right market for a service, providing a service through funded-projects, and leveraging digital technology to reach overseas consumers. The third section places its attention on the global trade policies that may help or hinder a firm's ability to compete in its home market and/or in the international market. Finally, the concluding chapter summarizes much of the main takeaways from each section. The conclusion goes further to highlight areas for future trade practices and policies as they pertain to the ever-growing and evolving international trade in services.

Bibliography

International Trade Centre. n.d. *Trade Map.* Accessed September 30, 2020. https://www.trademap.org/.

Hoekman, Bernard, and Carlos A. Primo Braga. 1997. *Protection and Trade in Services.* Washington, DC: The World Bank.

TRENDS IN INTERNATIONAL TRADE AND FOREIGN DIRECT INVESTMENT IN SERVICES

Chapter 2

Cross-border Trade in Services Is Not New!

"Do you know what blockchain technology is?" This is the question that was posed by the organizer of a small, private meeting composed of business and legal consultants in Downtown Los Angeles in 2017. For some sitting at the table, blockchain technology was a new concept. Blockchain technology is a digital ledger that allows for information sharing among authorized parties and eliminates a third-party or middleman who controls how information is distributed. Each person has access to the exact same information, which is impossible to copy or alter using this technology. The meeting organizer explained how blockchain technology had been introduced to the agricultural sector to enhance the tracking system applied to the whole supply chain from the farm to the table to ensure product safety. The technology also presented an opportunity for service providers in this meeting to collaborate and offer several services to farmers, especially in the Sub-Saharan African region, on developing their competitiveness in the U.S. market through the use of blockchain technology.

Blockchain technology is an important 21st-century innovation that is revolutionizing the way in which not only commodities, but services are offered both domestically and internationally. For example, the banking industry continues exploring ways in which the technology could improve efficiency and security in financial transactions in the global economy. In 2018, analysts predicted that companies, mainly in the area of financial services, would spend up to US$2.1 billion on blockchain technology, twice as much compared to the previous year (Mearian 2018). A year later, more company executives expressed that blockchain technology was among its top five priorities. However, only 23% of company executives actually began incorporating blockchain technology, down from 34% the year prior (Budman et al. 2019, 4).

Blockchain technology continues to have a tremendous impact on numerous global services-based industries. At the same time, it is important to understand that this technology is merely a part of a long line of innovative solutions for cross-border trade in services that go as far back as ancient history. In other words, although new technologies continue to appear that further facilitate the cross-border trade in services, the import and export of services have a long historical and sustainable track record, as in the areas of transportation, logistics, finance, and insurance.

Transportation and Logistics

Transportation services refer to companies that facilitate the movement of goods. Different modes of transport services include maritime shipping, trucking, freight rail, and air delivery. The movement of goods by sea accounts for 80–90% of the volume of international trade, according to the United Nations Conference on Trade and Development (UNCTAD) (United Nations 2018, 4). Generally speaking, shipping by ocean may be less expensive than by air and allows for the movement of a much larger volume of goods. Transport by sea has evolved since Ancient Egyptian civilization.

Around 3,000 BC, the shipping industry allowed for the movement of goods from one region to another throughout Africa, the Middle East, and Asia. The shipping industry was dominated by the ancient Egyptians because of their strong naval force. Egyptian ships evolved into larger, sturdier cargo ships made from wood, predominantly from imported cedar. As a result, the Egyptians could move a higher volume and heavier amount of cargo throughout North East Africa, the Mediterranean, and South Asia.

Eventually, the shipping industry became dominated by the Greeks, especially as pottery and gold were traded between mainland Greece and the Greek islands. The Greeks built ships to move goods throughout the Persian Empire.

Rome became a key player in maritime transport by the 8th century BC, during which it connected the West with southern India and other parts of Asia. The Roman civilization relied heavily on the import and export of goods. Key exports included cereals, wine, and olive oil. Imports consisted of precious metals, marble, and spices. Many goods in the Roman market, especially luxury silk goods, came from China (Galli 2017, 6–7). Commodities moved by land through the Silk Road or by water across the Indian Ocean. However, transport by land was often difficult due to the weak innovative land transport methods (Cartwright 2018). As a result, maritime transport operated much more quickly and cheaply. Ships often carried between 75 and 300 tons of goods (Cartwright 2018). Nevertheless, transport by ocean had its own set of risks such as dangerous weather conditions and piracy.

From the 15th to the 17th century, Spain, Portugal, the Netherlands, and Britain continued relying on both land and water transport to reach the Asian region, set up trading companies, and importing spices, silks, and cottons.

China controlled the trade routes throughout Southeast Asia going as far back as the 13th century, during which Marco Polo visited and documented China's strength in international commerce. Moving goods between China and the West required the use of shipping services. China often sent large ships carrying up to 120 tons of cargo across the Indian Ocean to engage in commerce with other parts of Asia, the Middle East, and East Africa. Many of these ships included sails made of bamboo to allow for durability and better steering (Griswold 2002). China sent 317 ships with 28,000 Chinese on a trade mission in 1405 (Griswold 2002). Developing its fleet of ships gave China the leverage to participate in international commerce, as well as promote political diplomacy and cultural exchanges. The Chinese economy grew as a result of these commercial, political, and cultural connections.

Britain has also historically relied heavily on maritime trade to build its economy. By the 17th century, Britain began bringing different commodities and resources from the Western Hemisphere, where it eventually began establishing colonies in what has been labeled North America, starting with Virginia, and throughout the part of the Caribbean region referred to as the West Indies. By 1686, over £1 million of goods, which included sugar, tobacco, and tropical foods, were shipped to London (Morgan 2011). Britain's exports to the colonies consisted mainly of woolen textiles.

Britain began buying and enslaving people from Africa, selling them as property to plantation owners, and forcing them to work on rice, tobacco, coffee, and sugar plantations throughout North and South America. Eventually, the enslaved peoples of Africa, most of whom were transported to the Caribbean region, far outnumbered the indigenous population that had been originally used for slave labor. The Transatlantic Slave Trade involved uprooting and transporting an estimated 12.5 million African peoples on a months-and miles-long journey across the Atlantic Ocean to the Americas (Cohen et al. 2017). The transport and trade of African peoples as commodities as a part of the system of slavery endured from the 15th to the 19th century. During the same time frame, 2.5–5 million Native Americans were enslaved (Cohen et al. 2017). By 1698, Britain was the top slave trader. Shipping services flourished and made such trades of goods and people across larger geographical regions possible.

Protectionism has been a part of the international shipping services industry, as evident during the 17th through the 19th centuries. Because shipping was an important industry for its economy, Britain implemented the Navigation Acts (1651–1854). The Navigation Acts were designed to restrict the trade of goods to English ships. Consequently, shipping costs increased. Nevertheless, the evolution of Britain's ships from the large sailing ships to those that made use of steam power, iron, and steel made maritime transport much faster and more reliable.

Whereas Asia connected with the West through the Silk Road, ocean transport became dominant for the region by the second half of the 19th century. As a result, the region emphasized the development of its ports and harbors. Japan grew into a significant trading partner with the world during the early part of the 20th century because of its naval strength.

Alternative methods of transporting goods around the world emerged. Eventually, cross-border land transport via railway and trucks emerged. The modern railway system began in Britain with the invention of the steam locomotive designed to transport passengers by the early 19th century. During the Industrial Revolution, the steam engine made it possible to ship goods at a lower shipping cost and with less risk of loss, compared to transport by waterway. Furthermore, the steam engine, in combination with the wider use of railroad tracks, made it possible for goods to be shipped over longer distances at a lower cost than that associated with the precursor—a wagon.

The rail system evolved to the use of freight trains, which moves cargo via freight cars that carry specific types of goods. The rail freight transport allows for the movement of goods more efficiently both in terms of time and use of energy. However, in the case of the United States, heavy government regulation made shipments by rail, particularly for manufactured products, more costly by the 1950 and 1960s, resulting in shippers turning toward delivery by highway ("A Short History of U.S. Freight Railroads" 2019). With the deregulation of the railroad industry by the 1980s, goods and foodstuffs could be transported efficiently. Even those goods that were shipped via maritime transport from one country to another still rely on rail freight transport services to transport large containers to the final destination within the latter country.

Trucking services also help to move goods across borders by land. During the 1930s, many commercial shipments in the United States were completed by truck, especially as roads underwent significant improvement due to the increased number of automobiles. Also, the enhancement and expansion of the U.S. highway system boosted the ability for the trucking industry to play a key role in commercial shipping (Minard 2015).

Notably, the rail and trucking systems are contemporary methods for land transport. Keep in mind that goods moved on land by caravan, which consisted of camels or horses, via the Silk Road. The transport of goods via the Silk Road for trading included long distances, slow movement, and, in many cases, a dangerous trek (Rodrigue et al. 2020). For this reason, the commodities that were traded via the Silk Road were limited to luxury goods such as silk, gold, jade, tea, and spices.

Finally, cargo could move across borders by air transport. The first demonstration of the effectiveness of air transport of goods across continents came during an international political crisis. Britain and the United States sent supplies, such as coal and foodstuffs, to West Berlin via the Berlin Airlift in response to the Soviet Union's blockade of West Berlin. The blockade lasted from June 24, 1948, to May 12, 1949. The peak daily amount of goods shipped via the Berlin Airlift reached 12,941 tons on April 15–16, 1949 (Grehan 2019, 157). The air cargo industry really grew following the deregulation of the airline industry in 1977. Private air freight carriers, such as United Parcel Service (UPS) and Federal Express (FedEx), grew and demonstrated the importance of air cargo to the airline industry.

A related services-based industry developed from the transport of commodities, which, in present times, is referred to as freight forwarding. The freight forwarder also handles the logistics associated with shipping a good by contracting with carriers to arrange large volumes of shipments, negotiate fares, assist with documentation, and track shipments. Today's freight forwarders have been labeled the "travel agent for freight" (Banker 2015). Freight forwarding goes as far back as one of the earlier formal business-to-business organizations established in 1836 by Thomas Meadows and Company Limited in London, England. The company used its local network of carriers to assist with transportation, documentation, and customs-related information.

It is important to mention that it has been recorded that the history of freight-forwarding actually extends earlier than the Thomas Meadows and Company Limited. The first group of freight forwarders were predominantly innkeepers who assisted their guests by holding and forwarding their personal belongings by the early 1800s ("The Rapid Evolving Freight Forwarding Industry" 2017; "What Is a Freight Forwarder" 2020). As mentioned, Thomas Meadows and Company Limited shifted freight-forwarding service into a business that has continued well into the next two centuries.

As the Industrial Revolution throughout Europe and United States during the 18th and 19th centuries resulted in a boom in manufacturing processes and manufactured goods, the need for a way to transport these goods safely to customers became important. Furthermore, the increased trade between Europe and North America increased the demand for freight forwarders.

According to the freight forwarding company Redwood Logistics:

> The purpose of freight forwarding has remained essentially the same throughout the centuries. Freight forwarders help get a customer's goods shipped safely to their chosen destinations. The means employed by freight forwarders has evolved over time to take advantage of the current technology to meet the demands of more shipping routes.

("The History of Freight Forwarding")

The freight forwarding industry has expanded and grown in countries all around the world. Freight forwarders do not physically move goods. Rather, they contract with carrier services to arrange shipping via ocean, land, and air and keep track of the shipment to ensure safe arrival to its point of destination.

Finance and Insurance

Another set of services-based industries that have historically played a key role in international trade are finance and insurance. These industries correspond with the need to pay for the international movement of goods and take proper measures to cover any losses. The barter system originally served as a form of payment before money was created. Bartering involves the exchange of services and goods for other services and goods in return.

Eventually, goods were originally financed through the bill of exchange—a private written order addressed by the seller to the buyer. The buyer, then, was required to pay on demand or a fixed amount by a specific time through a beneficiary. The bill of exchange system that is used today goes as far back as the 13th century. The bill of exchange became the system for financing international trade transactions. The Bank of England established the formal regulation of the bill of exchange system.

International trade finance experienced a downward trend as countries around the globe moved away from outward, open-market practices toward inward-looking protectionist strategies. In other words, trade barriers were used by numerous countries as a way of protecting local producers from foreign competition. The rise of protectionism meant the decline of the export of goods and, thus, a reduction in the need for international trade financing. Financial services rebounded during the latter half of the 20th century due to the resurgence of exports and credit requests. Various institutions, such as commercial banks and government agencies, offered export financing, credit insurance, and loan guarantees. Today, export financing is a key service that helps to boost trade now that sellers can get the required capital to produce, supply the needs of an overseas buyer, and reduce the risk of non-payment.

The insurance industry grew in significance to address the risks associated with the shipment of goods such as loss, damage, or theft. Insurance services go as far back as ancient civilization. Merchants in Babylon, Greece, and Rome relied on bottomry contracts, which were loans given to traders that did not have to be repaid should a shipment get lost at sea. The interest on the loan covered the insurance risk.

During the Medieval Period or Middle Ages (500 AD–1500 AD), sea loans were offered to merchants. These same merchants only repaid the sea loans upon safe arrival of a shipment. Additionally, merchants aimed to reduce their risk by spreading their cargo across several vessels. Placing goods on multiple ships presented its own set of challenges: 1) having to find more than one shipper going to the same destination, 2) having to negotiate multiple contracts, and 3) entrusting goods to more than one shipper (Kingston 2014, 2). Commenda contracts were another form of insurance during the medieval period, which emerged after Pope Gregory IX condemned the practice associated with sea loans. Under the sea loan arrangement, an individual would provide a traveling merchant with the capital necessary to ship goods with the agreement that both parties would share the profits. However, the financier bore the sea and commercial risk. The use of sea loans saw a decline beginning in 1236.

The contemporary insurance contract can be traced back to Italy during the mid-14th century. The risk associated with shipping goods internationally on a vessel shifted from the merchant to an underwriter upon the latter receiving a premium payment (Holdsworth 1917; Kingston 2014). Italian trade began to drop off, which created opportunities for cross-border underwriting services to other European countries. Nevertheless, the system established in Italy continued to influence the insurance industry.

By the 16th and 17th centuries, Britain, France, Holland, and Spain began to see the rise of their own local insurance industries. The first known insurance provider in England was Lloyd's of London. Edward Lloyd offered merchants with shipping information, which became known as Lloyd's List. In 1769, the list service evolved into a group of underwriters who provided marine insurance to merchants throughout Europe and America (Britannica). Marine insurance was mostly underwritten by one or more individuals. Eventually, individual providers began to specialize in the insurance business. Finally, formal companies emerged as providers of marine insurance (Clark 1978).

In the American colonies, individual persons began to get involved in the insurance trade (Murrey and Fensternaker 1990). Marine insurance became an important industry as America's exports increased more than fivefold from $20.2 million in 1790 to $108.3 million in 1807 (Murrey and Fensternaker 1990, 262). As a result, the number of firms increased dramatically. The Insurance Company of North America in Philadelphia became the first corporate insurance firm that formed in 1794.

Because of the transport of human beings destined for the system of slavery during the Transatlantic Slave Trade, these people were classified as commodities. Therefore, the cargo composed of human beings could be insured during a voyage, as argued in the 1783 court case of Gregson v. Gilbert. In this specific case, more than 130 enslaved Africans on the Zong, a British slave ship that was owned by the Gregson slave-trading syndicate, were murdered upon being thrown overboard. The ship's owners filed a claim for the loss of enslaved Africans, but the insurers refused to pay, because the loss was not due to accident or natural disaster. In the end, the court ruled the intentional killing of enslaved persons legal and ordered the insurers to cover the loss (Lobban 2007). Eventually, slave ships were no longer insured, and the slave trade was completely abolished in 1807.

As in Europe, the insurance industry saw a shift from individual to corporate underwriters. The latter could offer insurance services more efficiently and facilitate an easier payment and claim adjustment process to merchants (Clark 1978). The industry experienced significant loss in terms of payment of claims and reduced business during the 19th century. As several wars broke out during this period, such as the War of 1812 and the American Civil War, vessels were seized by the British and/or there was a significant decline in shipping. Insurance companies had to pay claims for such losses while having fewer clients (Murrey and Fensternaker 1990). The loss of vessels became less common resulting in the decrease in insurance rates (Clark 1978).

Innovative technologies in the 20th and 21st centuries have altered the way in which the services highlighted in this chapter are provided to allow for more efficiency and effectiveness, as well as enhanced security. For instance, with the introduction and growing use of online purchasing through e-commerce platforms as an additional option for brick and mortar retailers and online retailers, such as Amazon, shipping services have had to adapt to remain important and relevant. In 2018, about 1.8 billion people purchased goods online globally (Clement 2019). In 2019, e-retail sales reached $3.5 trillion dollars, up from $2.9 trillion dollars a year earlier. Online purchases represented 14.1% of retail sales around the world during the same year and are expected to increase to 22% by 2023 (eMarketer 2019). E-commerce allows companies to meet the demands of consumers who seek to purchase goods internationally and with quick delivery times. That can only be done with sophisticated delivery processes and systems to allow for faster delivery times, lower shipping costs, and flexibility in an ever-changing global business environment. As a result, the shipping industry has also had to evolve to meet the needs of the present-day consumer through the use of automation and artificial intelligence. Many logistics and transportation companies have also used outsourcing to third-party service providers for distribution, warehousing, and fulfillment. This model has become known as third-party logistics or 3PL. A 4PL company incorporates 3PL services plus manages the resources, technology, and infrastructure.

According to a representative from the ocean, truck, and rail freight forwarding 3PL company, BGI Worldwide Logistics:

> The logistics industry is continuously evolving to meet the demands of the changing marketplace. Companies are investing in advanced technology platforms and systems to handle the online retail boom with speed-to-market and the customer service experience becoming a major factor in company success. Organizations have had to quickly adapt by upgrading or implementing warehouse management systems to improve operations efficiency and flexibility, and by hiring employees with the technological training,

education, and soft skills to meet the new demands. Logistics companies must continue to innovate and adapt to changes in the market in order to remain relevant.

(Jackson 2018)

Automation has also played a significant role in the financial and insurance services industries. The ability to handle transactions online and respond to the needs of customers through online platforms allow for these service providers to move much more quickly to meet the needs of both local and international customers.

Digital technology continues to force industry-level changes, as in the case of the financial services industry, to meet the needs of a wider spectrum of customers. In 2018, 36% of consumers worldwide relied on e-wallet, which allows for payment for goods and services online through a computer or smartphone (Worldpay 2019). The Asia-Pacific region represented the area with the highest percentage of consumers using e-wallet at 52% and Latin America the smallest with 15% (Worldpay 2019). The digital wallet provides options for the percentage of the population that may find it difficult to open a bank account or get a loan. With the disruption to the system, the financial services are no longer just provided by traditional banks and credit unions but other providers such as tech giants Apple via Apple Pay and Google, Google Pay.

Blockchain technology is playing a role in revolutionizing the shipping and logistics industries. Blockchain technology benefited the maritime shipping industry by saving time in the process. For instance, shipping entails a document-intensive process. The documents include, but are not limited to, the following:

1. Bill of lading, a receipt listing all goods being shipped and indicates the owner of those goods;
2. Commercial invoice, which includes the value and information about goods being shipped for use during customs clearance and to determine duty rates for those goods;
3. Certificate of origin, which identifies the original place(s) of manufacture; and
4. Packing list, which describes weight and dimensions of the contents of a shipment.

The process varies in terms of time to complete all documents and the costs associated with exporting. For instance, according to the World Bank

Doing Business Survey, the documentary compliance process takes two hours to complete and costs US$60 to export from New York City (USA) to Canada. In the case of exporting from Mexico City to the United States, the documentary compliance process may take a bit longer—eight hours. Additionally, the cost is higher—US$100. Blockchain technology reduces the amount of time and lowers costs by utilizing a single blockchain with a ledger of information that can only be accessed by authorized parties to read, edit, and sign the blockchain ledger ("Can Blockchain Technology Bring Smooth Seas to Global Shipping?" 2018). Blockchain technology also reduces transit times, errors, and corruption. At the same time, blockchain technology increases transparency and improves regulatory compliance ("Can Blockchain Technology Bring Smooth Seas to Global Shipping?" 2018; Ogée and Furuya 2019; Pederson et al. 2019). The efficiencies and barrier removals created by blockchain technology have the potential to boost the volume of trade by 30% to US$1.1 trillion, according to World Economic Forum estimates in a 2018 white paper titled "Trade Tech – A New Age for Trade and Supply Chain Finance."

Blockchain is currently being used within the maritime shipping industry. For example, in 2018, Maersk, the largest container ship and vessel operator globally, and IBM, a multinational technology firm, formed a blockchain-enabled digital shipping platform—TradeLens. Other large companies—such as Hyundai Merchant Marine, a shipping company, and Samsung SDS, a subsidiary of the Samsung Group that provides information technology services—have also invested in blockchain technology. TradeLens has demonstrated the ability to cut administrative costs by up to 15% of the value of shipped goods, which translates to US$1.5 trillion worldwide (Comben and Rivet 2019). Even with this and other blockchain platforms, only 19.2% of logistics service providers have invested in blockchain technology (Ogée and Furuya 2019).

Notably, blockchain technology in maritime shipping carries several risks of its own. Having too many platforms without a common standard across the board may actually offset the benefit of efficiency ("Can Blockchain Technology" 2018). Whereas blockchain technology has been touted as increasing security, the real world has presented a different reality. Fraud and cybersecurity attacks through the use of blockchain technology have also plagued the maritime industry. For instance, the NotPetya cyberattack cost Maersk up to US$300 million and stalled its operations in 2017, a year prior to its development of TradeLens with IBM. Keep in mind that Maersk controls 76 ports all around the world and 800 vessels that include container ships responsible for carrying tons of cargo amounting to about one-fifth of global shipping capacity (Greenberg 2018). The company's whole computer system was shut down. Furthermore, employees received a message on their machines requesting payment in Bitcoin, a digital currency that also relies on blockchain technology, to release computer files. Bitcoin payment allows users to engage in transactions anonymously.

According to the World Economic Forum findings:

> Securing blockchain starts with traditional information security ... The distributed approach makes it much harder for attackers to tamper with information undetected. Given the number of inter- mediaries in global supply chains and the potential for theft and fraud, it is no surprise the industry is turning to blockchain.
>
> But when it comes to confidentiality and availability, blockchain can lag behind other technologies. It is absolutely not recom- mended to store sensitive information on blockchain for instance. Data availability and real-timeliness will also depend on the block- chain type: an in-theatre supply chain system for the military may not use the same blockchain type as a postal mail service.

(Ogée and Furuya 2019)

Most blockchain technology has been implemented in the financial services industry, specifically financial technology (fintech) (Budman et al. 2019, 3). The digital currency, Bitcoin, which relies on blockchain technology, emerged in 2009 as a response to the global financial crisis resulting from a decentralized banking system, in which some large banks engaged in uneth- ical lending practices.

Beyond digital currency, blockchain technology has been used to cre- ate a more efficient and secure financial services system. At the moment, the small- and medium-sized enterprises (SMEs) and emerging market economies bear the costs of a financial services system that still relies on traditional paper-based, manual processes, according to a World Economic Forum study ("Trade Tech" 2018). The same study argues that the digitization of the financial services industry helps to reduce processing times, waste, fraud, delays, and thus, costs. Simultaneously, transparency and security increases. Banks around the world have already started to implement block- chain technology as trade itself, as described above, becomes digitized. "Trade finance is an obvious area for blockchain technology. It is so old, it's done with fax machines, and you need a physical stamp on a piece of paper," says Charley Cooper, managing director of R3, in a 2017 interview with the *Financial Times* newspaper (Arnold 2017). R3 is a New York–based blockchain technology company.

Global managers in the services sector now have to adjust to the demands of consumers and embrace the shifts in technology. Global managers need to be forward thinking when it comes to the new technology and the lessons from these new technologies. The key lesson from the historical view is the long-term significance of the services sector going as far back as ancient times.

As we have seen, innovation gives rise to new industries in countries around the globe. As an interconnected globalized world, business services are now outsourced in a business-to-business (B2B) fashion, as exemplified with the rise of the call center industry in the 21st century thus, making other types of services tradable across borders.

A global manager's understanding of these changes is important as global customers seek faster, reliable, less costly services and a higher quality of life. In addition, the historical influences on the current trade in services should be an important part of international business training offered by the educational community and government agencies. Such an understanding by all stakeholders contributes to the global competitiveness of local firms and national economies.

Following that private meeting with professional service providers about blockchain technology, the technology itself continued to see growth in recent years. Time will tell what other innovations will emerge that may further revolutionize the services sector within the global economy. For now, global managers interested in the trade in services and policymakers seeking to develop policies that contribute to local competitive advantage should understand the trends in the import and export of services. Educators at business schools should also incorporate international trade, including in services, into their curriculum to truly begin preparing students to function in the current and ever-evolving global economy.

Bibliography

"A short history of U.S. freight railroads." n.d. Association of American Railroads. Accessed August 2, 2020. https://www.aar.org/wp-content/uploads/2020/08/AAR-Railroad-Short-History-Fact-Sheet.pdf.

Arnold, Martin. October 16, 2017. "Five ways banks are using blockchain." *Financial Times*. Accessed March 25, 2020. https://www.ft.com/content/615 b3bd8-97a9-11e7-a652-cde3f882dd7b.

Banker, Steve. 2015. *The Freight Forwarding Industry: The Times They Are a Changing*. Accessed March 11, 2020. https://www.forbes.com/sites/stevebanker /2015/09/21/the-freight-forwarding-industry-the-times-they-are-a-changing/# 7122d91a8c24.

Britannica. n.d. "Historical development of insurance." Accessed March 11, 2020. https://www.britannica.com/topic/insurance/Historical-development-of-insurance.

Budman, Matthew, Blythe Hurley, Abrar Khan, and Nairita Gangopadhyay. 2019. *Deloitte's 2019 Global Blockchain Survey: Blockchain Gets Down to Business*. Accessed March 22, 2020. https://www2.deloitte.com/content/dam/Deloitte/se/ Documents/risk/DI_2019-global-blockchain-survey.pdf.

Can Blockchain Technology Bring Smooth Seas to Global Shipping? n.d. Accessed March 18, 2020. https://worldview.stratfor.com/article/can-blockchain-techno logy-bring-smooth-seas-global-shipping.

Cartwright, Mark. 2018. "Trade in the Roman world." *Ancient History Encyclopedia*. Last modified April 12, 2018. https://www.ancient.eu/article/638/trade-in-the-ro man-world/.

Clark, John G. 1978. "Marine insurance in eighteenth-century La Rochelle." *French Historical Studies* 10 (4): 572–98.

Clement, J. 2019. E-commerce worldwide: Statistics & Facts. Accessed August 2, 2020. https://www.statista.com/topics/871/online-shopping/.

Cohen, Rhaina, Maggie Penman, Tara Boyle, and Shankar Vedantam. 2017. *An American Secret: The Untold Story of Native American Enslavement*. Washington, DC: National Public Radio.

Comben, Christina, and Coin Rivet. 2019. "Blockchain at sea: How technology is transforming the maritime industry." *Yahoo Finance*. Accessed March 22, 2020.

eMarketer. 2019. "E-commerce share of total global retail sales from 2015 to 2023." In *Statista*.

Galli, Marco. 2017. "Beyond frontiers: Ancient Rome and the Eurasian trade net-works." *Journal of Eurasian Studies* 8: 3–9.

Greenberg, Andy. 2018. "The untold story of Notpetya, the most devastating cyber-attack in history." *Wired*. Accessed March 22, 2020. https://www.wired.com/sto ry/notpetya-cyberattack-ukraine-russia-code-crashed-the-world/.

Grehan, John. 2019. *The Berlin Airlift: The World's Largest Ever Air Supply Operation, Images of Aviation*. South Yorkshire: Air World.

Griswold, Daniel. 2002. *Trade and the Transformation of China*. Washington, DC: Cato Institute.

Holdsworth, W. S. 1917. "The early history of the contract of insurance." *Columbia Law Review* 17 (2): 85–113.

Jackson, Sarita D. 2018. "Technological advances and their impact on logistics: A conversation with BGI worldwide logistics." Global Research Institute of International Trade Examiner, February 20, 2018. https://griit.org/?s=BGI.

Kingston, Christopher. 2014. "Governance and institutional change in marine insurance, 1350–1850." *European Review of Economic History* 18 (1): 1–18.

Lobban, Michael. 2007. "Slavery, insurance and the law." *Journal of Legal History* 28 (3): 319–28.

Mearian, Lucas. 2018. "Spending on blockchain technology to double this year to $2.1B." *Computer World*. Accessed August 1, 2020. https://www.computerworld .com/article/3251505/spending-on-blockchain-networks-to-double-this-year-to -21b.html.

Minard, Steve. 2015. "History of freight transportation." *Lojistic*. Accessed August 2, 2020. https://www.lojistic.com/blog/history-of-freight-transportation.

Morgan, Kenneth. 2011. "Symbiosis: Trade and the British empire." BBC. Accessed August 1, 2020. http://www.bbc.co.uk/history/british/empire_seapower/trade _empire_01.shtml.

Murrey, Jr., Joe H., and J. van Fensternaker. 1990. "Long-run profitability of fire and marine insurance companies: A 100-year study of Boston insurers." *Journal of Insurance Regulation* 9 (2): 259–73.

Ogée, Adrien, and Soichi Furuya. 2019. *Blockchain Is Becoming Key for Global Trade – But Is That a Gift for Hackers?* Geneva: World Economic Forum.

Pedersen, Asger B., Marten Risius, and Roman Beck. 2019. "A ten-step decision path to determine when to use blockchain technologies." *MIS Quarterly Executive*. 18(2): 1–17.

Rodrigue, Jean-Paul, et al. 2020. "The geography of transport systems." *Department of Global Studies and Geography*. Accessed August 1, 2020. https://transpo rtgeography.org/?page_id=1048.

The History of Freight Forwarding. n.d. Redwood Logistic. Accessed March 11, 2020. https://www.redwoodlogistics.com/the-history-of-freight-forwarding/.

The Rapid Evolving Freight Forwarding Industry. n.d. Mach1 Global Services, Inc. Accessed March 11, 2020. https://www.mach1global.com/rapid-evolving-freight -forwarding-industry/.

The World Bank. 2020. "Doing business survey: Measuring business regulations." Accessed March 11, 2020. https://www.doingbusiness.org/.

World Economic Forum and Bain & Company. *Trade Tech: A New Age for Trade and Supply Chain Finance.* 2018. Geneva: World Economic Forum. .

United Nations. 2018. *50 Years of Review of Maritime Transport, 1968–2018: Reflecting on the Past, Exploring the Future.* Geneva: United Nations Conference on Trade and Development (UNCTAD).

Thomas. "What is a freight forwarder and what do they do?". Accessed August 2, 2020. https://www.thomasnet.com/articles/services/freight-forwarding/.

Worldpay. 2019. "Share of selected payment methods as percentage of total e-commerce transaction volume worldwide in 2018, by region." Chart. *Statista*. Accessed August 2, 2020. https://www-statista-com.ezproxy.snhu.edu/statistics /348004/payment-method-usage-worldwide/.

Chapter 3

Global Trends in the New Economy

In 2020, many companies were forced to adjust rapidly as the global economy screeched to a halt in the wake of the coronavirus pandemic. As a result, a number of service providers had to turn toward alternative methods to continue to meet the needs of end users, especially in the areas of healthcare, finance, and education. The important role of digital technology over traditional approaches became evident, especially in the healthcare industry.

> This is because traditional processes—those that rely on people to function in the critical path of signal processing—are constrained by the rate at which we can train, organize, and deploy human labor. Moreover, traditional processes deliver decreasing returns as they scale. On the other hand, digital systems can be scaled up without such constraints, at virtually infinite rates.
>
> **(Wittbold et al. 2020)**

Cloud-based platforms, such as Cisco Webex, WhatsApp, and Zoom, offered their services worldwide to assist with maintaining crucial services such as healthcare, education, and finance.

This discussion about the importance of cross-border digital trade in services by no means intends to imply that person-to-person services are less important. The export of medical doctors to countries that lacked sufficient medical staff to address the quick spread of the coronavirus to a large number of people simultaneously was crucial, as in the case of Cuban doctors being sent to at least 14 countries by March 2020. Rather, digital technology allowed for important services to cross borders, regardless of any physical barriers.

This chapter shows the trends in terms of the global trade of services. The chapter goes further to highlight the top countries that export services to the world and what their top services exports include, the characteristics of firm-level service exporters, the impact on national economies, and the effects of the sector on the manufacturing and agricultural sectors.

The Continued Growth of Cross-border Trade in Services

Over the last two decades, the export of services has seen tremendous growth as consumers around the world seek faster, reliable, and less costly services. Additionally, the sector's growth results from the increased demand for leisure, educational, travel, healthcare, and other personal services (Rubalcaba 2013).

The services sector continues to outpace both the agricultural and industrial sectors in terms of the share of the world GDP. The services sector's share of global GDP increased from 61.6% in 1997 to 65% in 2017. On the contrary, the industrial sector (mining, manufacturing, and construction) accounted for 25.5% in 2017, down from 29.6% of world GDP in 1997. Agriculture's share of world GDP declined from 5.6% to 3.4% during the same 20-year period (Figure 3.1).

In terms of dollar value, global services exports reached US$5.8 trillion in 2018, an increase from US$5.2 trillion four years earlier, according to statistics collected from the International Trade Centre. The growth in international trade in services presents opportunities for countries to become globally integrated or to evolve in terms of their connection to the international market. In other words, the services sector plays a significant role for many countries in terms of competing internationally, more so than the traditional emphasis on agricultural and manufacturing sectors.

Top Service Exporters to the World

Business owners looking to expand to other markets often seek information on what countries are selling which goods and services to the global marketplace. Having such information helps a business to identify the best

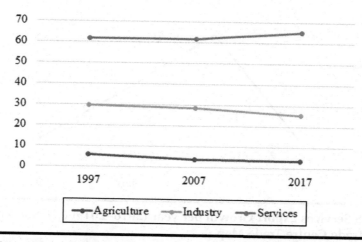

Figure 3.1 Share of world GDP by sector (1997–2017) (%). Source: World Bank, World Development Indicators

market(s) for its particular service, and national-level policymakers understand their countries' competitive advantage.

The United States is the number-one exporter of services to the world at US$828 billion, followed by the United Kingdom, US$376 billion; and Germany, US$331 billion, per the International Trade Centre. The top US services exports include travel and business services (Table 3.1).

The United States holds a global competitive advantage in these services exports. The annual growth rate for U.S. services exports to the world has ranged from 1.6% to 6.4% from 2016 to 2019 (Figure 3.2).

The top three markets for U.S. services exports are the European Union, US$243 billion; United Kingdom, US$69.6 billion; and Canada, US$58 billion.

Table 3.1 US Top Services Exports to the World (2018) (US$ thousand)

Service Label	Exported Value in 2018
All services	$828,428,111
Memo item: Commercial services	$808,224,066
Travel	$214,467,982
Other business services	$159,699,536
Charges for the use of intellectual property n.i.e.	$130,452,016
Financial services	$113,044,000
Transport	$92,304,000

Source: International Trade Centre Trade Map

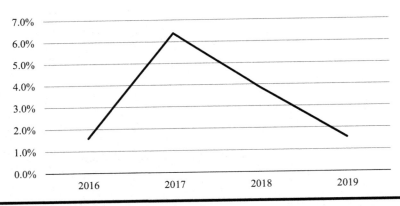

Figure 3.2   US Services Export Growth per year (2016–2019) (%). Source: International Trade Centre Trade Map

The change in the political and economic landscape with these three markets offers opportunities and risks for U.S. services-based companies exporting to these markets.

Types of Companies Exporting a Service

A 2009 study of U.S. services-based firms finds that those firms that export and enjoy consistent exposure to the international market tend to reap greater rewards. For instance, services exporters show a productivity value of 11.4; sales growth, 37.1%; and employment growth, 14.8% (Love and Mansury 2009, 635).

In the United States, small- and-medium-sized enterprises (SMEs), defined as having less than 500 US-based employees, "show higher total revenues, faster total revenue growth, and higher labor productivity than their non-exporting SME counterparts" (USITC 2010, i). More specifically, SME service exporters earned on average $3.8 million in 2017 compared to $1 million for the non-exporting SME service providers. SME services exporters experienced on average a 32.3% growth in revenue compared to 23.6% for the non-exporters from 2002 to 2007. During the same time period, the services SME exporters saw a 43.5% increase in labor productivity compared to only 26.8% for those SME service providers that do not export (USITC 2010, xii).

These SMEs access foreign markets through direct exports compared to the larger firms that sell both goods and services overseas through foreign affiliates. Although SMEs and SME multinational companies that export a service are in the minority, they tend to rely much more heavily on exports than do their large service-exporting counterparts.

The European Union remains the top regional exporter of services. With deeper trade liberalization in the European Union, larger, multinational enterprises have replaced the SME service providers, especially in hotel and financial services (Eurostat 2019).

Latin America and the Caribbean also export a significant amount of services worldwide. Many regional SMEs rely on service-based industries to expand and give them a competitive advantage (FEDEX 2017; UPS 2018). More specifically, the logistics industry remains crucial for many of these SME exporters because of customer demand for quicker and less costly deliveries.

Effect on National Economies

By the 18th through the 20th centuries, economists and policymakers around the world emphasized the shifting from an agriculture-based economy to an industrial one to achieve economic growth and global competitiveness. For example, the United States and Western Europe embarked upon the First Industrial Revolution, which transformed these economies. Real incomes increased quickly and far surpassed those of the countries that were not industrialized. According to earlier calculations, the average income in the United States was six times the world average and for Western Europe, more than two times the world average (Deane 1957). On the opposite end of the spectrum, per capita incomes for the Latin American region accounted for only two-thirds of the world average. Per capita incomes in Asia and Africa reached less than 25% of the world average (Deane 1957). The huge economic gap between the industrialized and non-industrialized countries demonstrated the link between industrialization, international competitiveness, and economic growth.

The larger Latin American countries followed suit with policies that allow many to shift from being solely an agriculture-based economy toward an industrialized one. During this period, many Latin American countries relied on high tariff rates, low quotas, and import licenses to protect local manufacturers from foreign competition in the home market. Some Asian countries also shifted toward an industrialized economy through protectionist practices but with an emphasis on exporting those goods for which they had a comparative advantage.

The 21st century continues to present a completely different landscape for economies and industries. A number of countries are able to leap from a predominantly agriculture-based economy to a larger services-based one, according to a *Deloitte Insights* report (see Buckley and Majumdar 2018).

For instance, in 2018, India's services sector accounted for 49% of its GDP compared to 31% five decades earlier. Fifty-seven percent of Sri Lanka's GDP comes from its services sector up from 47% in 1968, according to statistics collected from the World Bank. The increasingly contributing role that the services sector plays in national economies also reveals the changes in production, output, and employment. It is these changing dynamics that global managers and policymakers must be aware of.

The services sector of several developing countries, led by Luxembourg, St. Lucia, Malta, Lebanon, and the Turks and Caicos Islands, represents 70% of global GDP, according to World Bank statistics. These figures illustrate the many economies that are developing their services sectors, thereby contributing to a different economic make-up in terms of production, output, and employment, that global managers and policymakers must be aware of.

The small European country of Luxembourg exemplifies the important role that the services sector plays in its domestic composition and international competitiveness. The services sector represents 79% of Luxembourg's GDP. Close to 90% of Luxembourg's population is employed in the services sector, and the value added per worker reached US$203,000 in 2018 (The World Bank 2020; World Bank World Development Indicators). As a services-based economy, Luxembourg continues to experience a healthy economy with a GDP growth rate of 3.72%; inflation rate, 1.8%; and unemployment rate, 5.2% in 2019 (MarketLine 2019). The large services sector has contributed to the economic growth and development of the small country.

Additionally, Luxembourg's services sector has allowed the country to become globally integrated and competitive. The country has a trade surplus in its services trade with the world of about US$27 billion, which has grown steadily since 2014. The majority of Luxembourg's services exports go to the European Union and throughout the rest of Europe, with Germany and the United Kingdom being its top European markets. Most of its services exports consist of financial services. The case of Luxembourg demonstrates that smaller developing economies can actively and successfully engage in the global economy through the services sector.

The regions in which their services sector contributes the most to the global GDP are the European Union and Latin America and the Caribbean. These regions' services sectors account for 60% of the global GDP. The high contribution of the services sector demonstrates the importance of the sector in their economic growth (Figure 3.3).

The services sector presents employment opportunities in countries worldwide. Just over 50% of employment around the world can be attributed

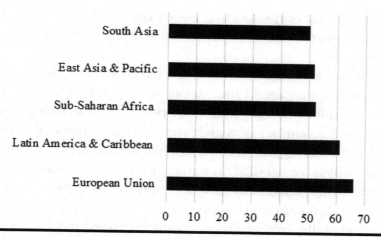

Figure 3.3 Share of Services GDP by region (2018) (%).* Source: World Bank, World Development Indicators

to the services sector (UNCTAD 2018). The value added per worker from the services sector in the European Union reached US$79,000 and that of Latin America reached US$19,000 in 2018. As a result, governments and educational institutions throughout these regions would benefit from developing its workforce to meet the demand for services for the global community.

At the same time, the results for the top regional service exporters have highlighted challenges in terms of productivity. The European Union has experienced slow or declining growth in productivity and lower cross-border investment in services compared to goods, which can be attributed to "regulatory restrictions and costly administrative procedures" (European Commission 2017, 1). The Latin American region has also experienced slow growth in the services sector, with the exception of telecommunications. A 2013 Inter-American Development Bank report suggests developing policies and practices that emphasize innovation in the services sector (Rubalcaba 2013). Policymakers become instrumental in developing rules, practices, etc., that impact the services sector and thus take into account the effect of their policies and ways to promote innovation to support a globally competitive services sector, which, in turn, contributes to domestic economic growth and productivity.

At the country level, in some cases, the results actually showed higher levels of productivity, as in the case of Turkey, an emerging market economy. From 2003 to 2015, Turkish services exporters showed far more labor

---

* Figures for the North American and the Middle East and North African (MENA) regions for 2018 are not available.

productivity than their non-exporting counterparts (Dincer and Tekin-Koru 2019). Services exporters' labor productivity aligned with that of the manu-facturing exporters.

Other countries, as in the case of India, have benefited from develop-ing a comparative advantage in the export of certain types of services, which transformed its economy and labor pool. The rise in the call center industry presented a number of higher skilled employment opportunities in India that also offered higher pay. "[W]hile call center jobs are often por-trayed as 'low-skilled' or 'clerical' in nature, they in fact require considerable knowledge and skills" (Batt et al. 2005). According to a 2005 study, workers with high school diplomas and college degrees benefitted from developing English-language skills, cross-cultural communication, and a deeper under-standing of the product, service, and technical systems. Many of these same employees had to undergo an average of six weeks of training, although it would take about three months to become proficient in the language, etc., in international call centers (Batt et al. 2005).

Indian workers who spoke English found it easier to secure employment much quicker and were paid relatively high wages. During the Indian call center industry boom, employees earned 30% more than those working for domestic call centers. The average yearly pay reached US$2,687 for interna-tional call centers compared to US$2,108 for domestic call centers in 2004 (Batt et al. 2005, 18). The managers in the international call centers also earned more at US$8,638 compared to their counterparts in the domestic call centers. In addition to skill development, the international call center industry led to the growth of "transnational labor," in which local processes, capital, and cultural values are influenced by international forces (McMillin 2006).

The services sector has played a greater role in India's economy. The services sector (value-added) accounts for 49% of India's GDP, yet only 7.4% of its economic growth, according to World Bank statistics. Furthermore, although the types of services described here may have transformed the labor pool, the services sector only employs just a little over 30% of the Indian population (Plecher 2020a). India's total services exports to the world grew slightly more than 30% from 2014 to 2018, per data collected from the International Trade Centre. Most of those services were in the areas of com-mercial, business, and telecommunication services.

In recent years, Mexico has become competitive in the international call center industry. U.S. immigration policy has contributed to the availability of a group of bilingual and bicultural employees who could offer business services to U.S. customers.

Historically, India has been the call center capital of the world. But Tijuana has been able to lure call centers away from India because of the city's availability of accent-neutral English speakers and Mexico's low wages relative to those of the United States.

(Solis 2019)

The ability of many to speak English very well and fully comprehend American culture, as well as the lower costs and geographical proximity, has provided Mexico with a competitive advantage in the call center industry. As a result, Mexico has been ranked number three in the world and first in Latin America as a competitive market for the call center services industry (*Competitividad Global de la Industria de Centros de Contacto* 2018). Of the total call centers in Mexico, 91% are Mexican owned and their business is mainly with the United States and Canada (*Censo Nacional de Centros de Contacto* 2018). The industry is expected to continue to grow in Mexico, especially since opportunities arise for expansion throughout Latin America, as well as other regions such as Europe and Asia. Customers based in Europe and the Asia-Pacific account for 17% and 7% of Mexico's international call center operations, respectively (*Censo Nacional de Centros de Contacto* 2018). The call centers present employment opportunities and higher wages in different cities in Mexico, as in the case of Tijuana.

Unlike India, the majority of Mexico's workforce is employed in the services sector. About 61% of the Mexican population is employed in the services sector, compared to close to 13% in agriculture and 26%, industry (mining, manufacturing, construction) (Plecher 2020b). At the same time, the sector contributes to 63% of Mexico's GDP.

Whereas developing and emerging economies may benefit to some degree from outsourcing services, the threat of competition from lower-cost service providers remains.

Interlinkages among the Services, Manufacturing, and Agricultural Sectors

The services, manufacturing, and agricultural sectors are not mutually exclusive. Rather, many services industries support the other two sectors. The integration of services into manufacturing and agriculture has contributed to the growth of the sector (Rubalcaba 2013).

As internationalization requires that businesses differentiate themselves to remain competitive, many manufactured products incorporate value-added services. For example, the call center industry discussed earlier provides value to customers through 24-hour technical support for products that have been purchased, such as a computer. Buying technological products and equipment also comes with value-added services such as local tech support, warranties, delivery, and credit and insurance services, all of which come with an additional labor pool and costs for the consumer.

The movement of both agricultural and manufactured goods depends on transportation and logistical services. The interconnected relationship became apparent in 2020 when protectionist practices banning the export of personal protective equipment and certain pharmaceuticals in response to the coronavirus and high tariffs on these imports due to the U.S.-China trade war resulted in a drop in the volume of trade. As a consequence, many freight-forwarding companies and port services experienced a slowdown.

Simultaneously, other services, such as telecommunications, saw exponential growth in 2020 with the help of digital technology. During the global economic paralysis resulting from the health pandemic, telecommunications services that relied on digital technology aided in the even faster export of some key services such as healthcare, education, and finance. These services could still be exported without worrying about any physical or tariff barriers. However, regulatory barriers can present a challenge to services providers, as in the case of tighter rules toward foreign direct investment imposed by specific countries during the health crisis.

Overall, the global trend in the new economy has seen the rise in various types of cross-border services. The United States remains the number-one services exporter to the world, and many SMEs play a key role in the global export of services. The impact of services exports has varying results on national economies in terms of GDP growth and productivity. Finally, the growth of the services sector has the potential to contribute to the growth and productivity across other sectors. With this information, policymakers and educators can develop programs that enhance the competitive advantage of its service-based providers in the global market, which, in turn, can contribute to the growth of the national economy.

Bibliography

Batt, Rosemary; Virginia Doellgast; Hyunji Kwon; Mudit Nopany; Priti Nopany; and Anil da Costa. 2005. "The Indian call centre industry: National benchmarking report strategy, HR practices, & performance. In *CAHRS* Working Paper *Series*. New York: Cornell University.

Buckley, Patricia; and Rumki Majumdar. 2018. *The Services Powerhouse: Increasingly Vital to World Economic Growth: Issues by the Numbers*. Stamford: Deloitte Insights.

Censo Nacional de Centros de Contacto. n.d. In *BPO-KPO/ITO 2017.* http://imt .com.mx/wp-content/uploads/2018/03/CENSO-NACIONAL.pdf.

Competitividad Global de la Industria de Centros de Contacto. n.d. In *BPO-KPO/ ITO 2a Edición*. http://imt.com.mx/wp-content/uploads/2018/02/Competitiv idad-Global.pdf.

Deane, Phillis. 1957. "The industrial revolution and economic growth: The evidence of early british national income estimates." *Economic Development and Cultural Change* 5 (2):159–174.

Dincer, Nergiz; and Ayca Tekin-Koru. 2019. "An anatomy of firm-level productivity in Turkey in the AKP era." In Working Papers. Giza: Economic Research Forum.

European Commission. 2017. *European Semester Thematic Factsheet Services Markets*. https://ec.europa.eu/info/sites/info/files/file_import/european-semest er_thematic-factsheet_services-markets_en.pdf.

Eurostat. 2019. International trade in services by types of service: Statistics Explained. Accessed April 19, 2020. https://ec.europa.eu/eurostat/statisticsexpla ined/.

FEDEX. 2017. "FEDEX study indicates SMEs in Latin America continue to show growth and optimism." Accessed April 19. https://newsroom.fedex.com/newsroom/fedex -study-indicates-smes-latin-america-continue-show-growth-optimism/.

International Trade Centre. n.d. *Trade* Map. https://www.trademap.org/.

Love, James H.; and Mica Ariana Mansury. 2009. "International business review." In *Exporting and Productivity in Business Services: Evidence from the United States*, 18: 630–642.

MarketLine. 2019. Luxembourg In-depth PESTLE insights. Retrived from MarketLine database.

McMillin, Divya C. 2006. "Outsourcing identities: Call centres and cultural transformation in india." *Economic and Political Weekly* 41 (3):235–241.

Plecher, H. 2020a. *Distribution of the Work Force across Sectors in India 2019*. Hamburg: Statista.

Plecher, H. 2020b. *Distribution of the Workforce across Economic Sectors in Mexico 2019*. Hamburg: Statista.

Rubalcaba, Luis. 2013. "Innovation and the new service economy in Latin America and the Caribbean." In *Regional Policy Dialogue*. Washington, DC: Inter-American Development Bank.

Solis, Gustavo. 2019. "Tijuana's call centers offer a lifeline to deportees struggling to live in Mexico." *Los Angeles Times.* Accessed August 7, 2020.

The World Bank. 2020. *Luxembourg: Distribution of employment by economic sector from 2009 to 2019.* Hamburg: Statista.

The World Bank. n.d. World Development Indicators. https://databank.worldbank .org/source/world-development-indicators.

United Nations Conference on Trade and Development (UNCTAD). 2018. *Trade in Services and Employment.* New York, NY: United Nations.

UPS. 2018. "UPS Study Reveals Main Trends Into the Import and Export Behavior of Small and Medium Sized Exporters and Importers in Latin America." *UPS Pressroom.* Accessed April 19. https://pressroom.ups.com/pressroom/Cont entDetailsViewer.page?ConceptType=PressReleases&id=1539093959922-644.

USITC (U.S. International Trade Commission). 2010. *Small and Medium-sized Enterprises: Characteristics and Performance.* Washington, DC: USITC.

Wittbold, Kelley A.; Colleen Carroll; Marco Lansiti; Haipeng Mark Zhang; and Adam B. Landman. 2020. "How hospitals are using AI to battle Covid-19. *Harvard Business Review.* Accessed April 6, 2020. https://hbr.org/2020/04/how-hospitals -are-using-ai-to-battle-covid-19.

Chapter 4

Foreign Direct Investment in Services

The value of digital technology in allowing for services to transcend tariff and other physical barriers benefits both developed and developing economies. As mentioned in the previous chapter, digital technology is merely a mechanism for cross-border interaction and transactions. Digital technology does not address the underlying inequalities in terms of access to computers, the internet, and wireless services. Consequently, a good portion of the global population faces a digital deficit, in which access to crucial services that are provided digitally, such as education, healthcare, financing, and communication, remains highly limited. Foreign direct investment (FDI) in narrowing the digital divide is one way to expand the reach of cross-border trade in services. For the purpose of this chapter, FDI is defined as an investor setting up, buying, or maintaining a controlling share of a company in a country different from the home country. Several factors contribute to a country's ability to attract FDI such as political stability and security, liberal trade policies toward investment, an open and transparent business environment, and a large domestic market. This chapter looks at recent trends for FDI in the services sector in general, factors that contribute to attracting FDI, the impact of such FDI on domestic economies, and the implications for both the business and policymaking communities.

FDI Inbound and Outbound Global Trends in Services

FDI Inbound

In many countries, FDI in the services sector has surpassed that of the manufacturing sector, which demonstrates the significance of the sector to the global economy. The number-one recipient of net FDI is the United States. The United Kingdom and Canada account for the top two sources of FDI for the United States (Organization for International Investment [OFII] 2018, McPhillips 2019). China is the largest emerging economic investor in the United States with close to US$60 billion. FDI from China jumped more than 300% from 2012 to 2017, according to data collected from the Organization for International Investment (OFII). Total global inflows in the United States reached US$251 billion in 2019, slightly less than the US$254 reported a year earlier, according to the March 2020 International Trade Administration (ITA) report, titled "Global Outlook: United States Remains the Largest Destination for FDI in the World." Based on findings by the United Nations Conference on Trade and Development (UNCTAD), more than 90% of FDI inflows into the United States go toward acquisitions. Greenfield FDI, a type of investment in which a parent company establishes a subsidiary in another country, has shown a 27% increase from 2018 to 2019, per the same ITA report. Most of its greenfield investments are in real estate, rental and leasing services, alongside manufacturing, both with a value of US$2.6 billion, per the Bureau of Economic Analysis.

In terms of FDI stock, the majority goes toward the U.S. manufacturing sector. Nevertheless, many services-based industries have also benefited greatly from FDI, especially the finance and insurance industries, which received just under US$540 billion in 2017 (OFII 2018).

OECD data shows that Luxembourg receives the most inward FDI stocks in services, which far surpasses FDI stocks in its manufacturing sector.* Upon a closer look at the FDI stock in services alone among OECD countries, Luxembourg remains the number-one recipient. In fact, FDI stocks in services for Luxembourg far outweighs that of its manufacturing sector. In 2018, Luxembourg, which was highlighted in Chapter 3 as being a significant contributor to the global GDP via its services sector, reported FDI stock of US$3.8 trillion (Figure 4.1).

---

* Per the OECD definition and measurement, inward FDI stocks in the services sector refers to the total amount of direct investment in the economy being highlighted at the end of the year and includes the value of foreign investors' equity in and the net loans received by reporting economy.

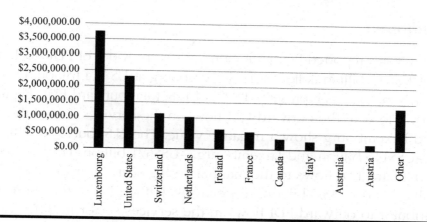

Figure 4.1 Top 10 recipients of inward FDI stocks in services (2018) (US$million).
Source: Organization for Economic Cooperation and Development (OECD)

Manufacturing, on the other hand, only received US$3.7 billion. The country's inward FDI stocks in services represented 99.9% of the total FDI.

However, when we look at inward FDI flows in the services sector, the United States remains the top recipient with a value of US$81 billion. Nevertheless, the U.S. manufacturing sector still receives a greater share of the FDI flows (Figure 4.2).

Luxembourg, which is not listed in the figure below, reported negative FDI inflows of −US$387 billion in 2018.

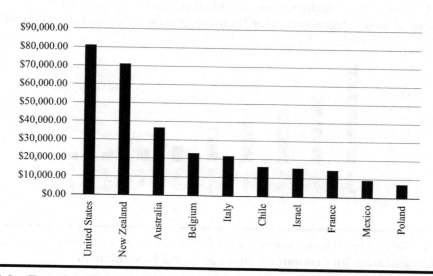

Figure 4.2 Top 10 recipients of inward FDI flows in services (2018) (US$million).
Source: Organization for Economic Cooperation and Development (OECD)

FDI Outbound

The United States reported being the number-one provider of FDI stocks in services with US$4.9 billion, followed by Luxembourg at US$4.4 trillion. FDI outward stocks* in services represented 82% of U.S. total outward FDI (Figure 4.3).

When we look at the outward FDI flows in the services sector, the United States and Luxembourg show a negative value. The U.S. outward FDI flows reached −US$136 billion and Luxembourg, −US$371 billion. For both countries, its outward FDI flows to the manufacturing sector remained positive at US$51 billion and US$3.8 billion, respectively. Rather, Japan represented the top contributor to outward FDI flows in the services sector in 2018 with a value of US$71.7 billion (Figure 4.4).

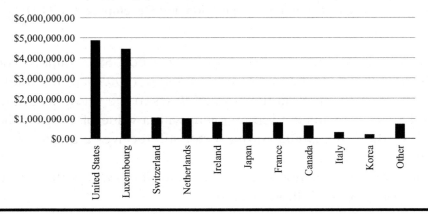

Figure 4.3 Top 10 contributors of outward FDI stocks in services (2018) (US$million). Source: Organization for Economic Cooperation and Development

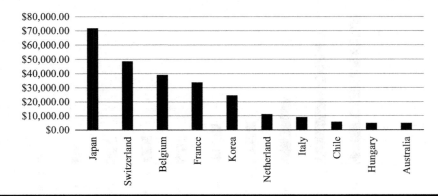

Figure 4.4 Top 10 contributors to outward FDI flows in services (2018) (US$million). Source: Organization for Economic Cooperation and Development

* Per the OECD definition and measurement, outward FDI stocks are "the value of the resident investors' equity in and net loans to enterprises in foreign economies" (OECD 2020).

However, the economy changed drastically in 2020 as a result of the global health pandemic caused by COVID-19. The coronavirus pandemic truly caused a disruption in the global economy to the point that FDI flows across borders dropped dramatically. The UNCTAD estimates that FDI in developing and emerging economies will decrease by 16%. Overall, in its March 2020 Investment Trends Monitor report, FDI was expected to decrease anywhere from 5 to 15%, a change from earlier predictions of marginal growth from 2020 to 2021. By early May 2020, the OECD reported in *Foreign Direct Investment Flows in the Time of COVID-19* an estimate of a 30% decline in global FDI, as the best-case scenario. The drop in FDI would be far greater for developing countries. By June, the UNCTAD World Investment Report anticipated an even higher drop in global FDI. FDI flows globally are expected to drop by 40% to under US$1 trillion for the first time since 2005. In 2019, global FDI flows reached US$1.54 trillion. Furthermore, the same report indicates that FDI is estimated to decline by another 5–10% in 2021 and start to recover by 2022.

Even in the midst of the global economic slowdown, FDI in certain industries still grew. Digital technology produced more than half of the investment in the first couple of weeks in March, according to an *FDI Intelligence* report (Dettoni 2020). "FDI in the digital sector is on the rise, including software, data centres and R&D … In 2017, this type of FDI ranked highest in number of projects and third in number of jobs created" (Maister 2020).

Other services-based industries still experienced a growth in earnings, such as healthcare, technology, and communication. The services sector in different countries continued to attract FDI inflows in 2020, as in the case of India. The *Financial Express* reports that India's services sector received up to US$7.8 billion in FDI inflows, a 17% increase, in FY 2020 (Sharma 2020). The types of services industries that saw FDI inflow growth in India in FY 2020 consist of finance, banking, insurance, research and development, testing, analysis, and outsourcing (Keelery 2020).

FDI Flows in Services by Group of Economies

Shifting the focus toward FDI inflows for types of economies varies among groups of economies—developed, economies in transition, and developing. FDI inflows declined for developed economies within the last year, according to the 2020 UNCTAD World Investment Report. On the other hand, economies in transition showed growth in the amount of FDI that they attracted within the last year. Transition economies refer to those economies that are in the process of shifting from a predominantly state-run economy toward a market-oriented one. Developing economies also enjoyed an increase in FDI inflows in recent years.

Developed economies

Developed economies experienced a 27% drop from 2017 to 2018 and a 6% decrease from 2018 to 2019 (UNCTAD World Investment Report, 2019c and 2020c).

However, the earlier trends for FDI inflows in services for developed economies have shown opposite results overall for these same economies over a four-year period from 2014 to 2018. For example, the top three developed OECD economies that recently received the most FDI inflows in services—United States, Netherlands, and Australia—saw a combined increase of 794% from US$21 billion in 2014 to US$189 billion in 2018 (Figure 4.5).

Six of the reported OECD developed economies showed a decrease to the point of reporting negative FDI inflows in services in 2018. Those economies included Finland, –US$263 million; Iceland, –US$428 million; Japan, –US$3.9 billion; Switzerland, –US$28.4 billion; Ireland, –US$93 billion; and Luxembourg, –US$387 billion.

Economies in transition

Economies in transition received a 65% increase in FDI inflows (UNCTAD Investment Trends Monitor 2020). According to a 2007 World Bank report on the economies in transition throughout Eastern Europe and Central Asia, high-quality services, such as transport or telecommunications, play a

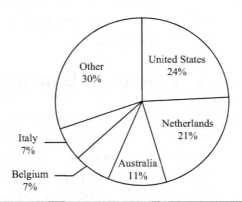

Figure 4.5 Top five OECD-developed economy recipient of FDI inflows for services (2018) (%). Source: OECD Data

significant role in attracting FDI (Fernandes 2007, 3). Countries that implemented policy reforms resulting in a more efficient services sector since the 1990s attracted more FDI and saw faster per capita GDP growth (Fernandes 2007, 3).

Developing economies

On the other hand, FDI flows to developing economies saw a 2% increase from 2017 to 2018, and their share of global FDI jumped up by 54%. Developing economic FDI inflows remained the same from 2018 to 2019. Although global FDI has shown "anemic growth since 2018," international production has continued to grow due to cross-border trade of services, as well as royalties and licensing fees (UNCTAD 2019).

In terms of OECD developing economies, FDI inward flows in services increased by 76% from 2014 to 2018. Israel showed the greatest increase from US$4.8 billion to US$15 billion during this time period (Figure 4.6).

FDI by Region and Key Opportunities

Africa

According to a 2019 UNCTAD report, the African continent has seen overall increases in FDI, which countered much lower expectations. Whereas FDI declined for a number of countries around the world from 2017 to 2018, the African region's FDI increased by 11% during the same period to US$46 billion. For the Sub-Saharan African region alone, FDI increased by 13% to

Figure 4.6 FDI inflows to the services sector in OECD developing countries (2018). (%) Source: OECD Data

$32 billion. The largest investor in Africa by 2017 was France, followed by the Netherlands, the United States, the United Kingdom, and China, as an increase in demand along with a jump in the price of commodities mainly produced in Africa. Shortly after, China has become the number-one investor in Africa in terms of capital and jobs created (Figure 4.7).

The United States has the most number of projects on the continent, according to a 2018 Africa Attractiveness report published by EY (formerly known as Ernst and Young) (EY 2018) (Figure 4.8).

Egypt receives the most amount of investment in terms of jobs and capital. In 2018, 32,000 jobs were created in Egypt, and it received a capital investment of $12 billion. South Africa ranks number one in terms of being the recipient of foreign-led projects followed by Egypt.

The majority of the FDI vis-à-vis projects and jobs were in the services and industry sectors. FDI capital went to extractives, 36%. In Egypt,

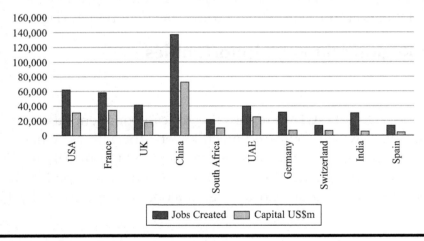

Figure 4.7   FDI to African continent by country (2018). Source: EY

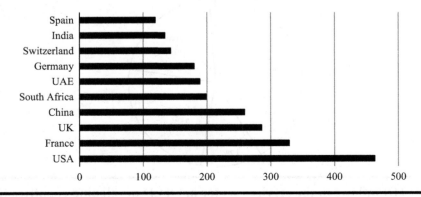

Figure 4.8   FDI projects in Africa (2018). Source: Brookings Institute

the main attractor of FDI in the region, private sector reforms, including increased protection for investors, has resulted in investment in the banking and financial sectors.

The same 2019 UNCTAD report, "Foreign Direct Investment to Africa Defies Global Slump, Rises 11%," finds that investment in both goods and services for the continent remains stable. However, most of the investment is concentrated in specific countries in Northern and Southern Africa, as well as the emerging manufacturing hubs in East Africa. For the African continent, as a whole, opportunities in investment beyond its natural resources sectors or manufacturing rest with services-based industries such as tourism, telecommunications, transportation, and medical (*South Africa: Foreign Investment* 2020, Hoekman 2018, Newfarmer et al. 2018). Financial and insurance services, real estate, and business services represent the top sectors that receive FDI in South Africa. The latest available data shows that these services represented 45% of the total FDI in 2017 (*South Africa: Foreign Investment* 2020). Other sub-Saharan African countries, such as Rwanda, has attracted 47% of FDI between 2008 and 2011. Rwanda now offers 21st-century mobile technology, which allows for increased phone subscriptions and use of mobile payment services. Other key services, such as payment of taxes, shifted to digital platforms (Spray and Wolf 2018).

Asia*

Overall, the region, which also includes some of the Asia-Pacific countries, shows higher inward FDI flows than outward flows. Furthermore, both inward and outward FDI flows have surpassed that of other sectors, including the manufacturing sector (Figure 4.9).

The United States remains the number-one investor throughout the region, except when it comes to the low-income Asian countries. For the latter, Malaysia and India have been the top sources of FDI (Kirkegaard 2012, 14). Financial services, construction and real estate, and transportation services were the top three services that attracted FDI to the Asian region from 1988 to 2011.

The services sector attracted the largest amount of FDI—66% between 2014 and 2018—within the Association of Southeast Asian Nations (ASEAN) member countries, according to the *ASEAN Investment Report*.

---

* Asia refers to the member countries of the Asian Development Bank, which also includes the Asia-Pacific countries.

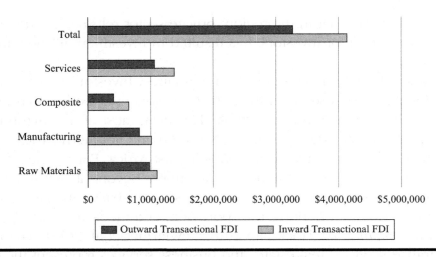

Figure 4.9 Transactional FDI Asia 1988–2011 (US$million) (by sector.) Source: Kirkegaard (2012)

According to UNCTAD's 2019 *World Investment Report*, Asia received the most amount of FDI at 39% of total world inflows in 2018. That percentage increased from 33% a year prior. Hong Kong (China) FDI inflows saw a 4% increase from 2017 to 2018, mostly attributed to the services sector. FDI inflows for the Southeast Asian region also witnessed growth in its FDI inflow, especially in financial, retail and wholesale trade, and digital trade. In South Asia, India received the most FDI inflows, which went to communication and financial services, as well as manufacturing and cross-border mergers and acquisitions.

Many countries throughout Asia, especially Southeast Asia, have seen significant economic growth that they have also become a source of FDI to other countries. The greatest source of FDI altogether for the Asian region comes from Singapore, located in Southeast Asia. Singapore contributes just under US$15 billion in FDI to the Asian region. Japan, Hong Kong, and China follow in the fifth, sixth, and seventh places with US$3.2 billion, US$694 million, and US$160 million, respectively (Chakraborty 2020).

FDI inflows to the region go predominantly toward the services sector due to the numerous growing opportunities in finance, banking, insurance, outsourcing, and research and development. The services sector has attracted US$7.9 billion worth of investments. Computer, software, and hardware followed with US$7.7 billion; telecommunication with US$4.6 billion; trading with US$4.4 billion; and the automobile industrywith US$2.8 billion. The services sector accounts for the largest portion of FDI in the areas just mentioned at 29% (Figure 4.10).

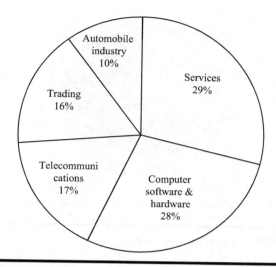

Figure 4.10 FDI inflows by sector to Asia (2019–20) (%). Source: Chakraborty (2020)

Europe

The services sector represented 84.6% of inward FDI stocks, measured at the end of a given year, for EU-28 by the end of 2016, according to Eurostat. Close to 85% of EU-28 inward FDI stocks go toward the services sector, per data collected from Eurostat. These services include financial and insurance; professional, scientific, and technical activities; distributive trades; information and communication; administrative and support; real estate; transportation and storage; and accommodation and food services. The United States remains the top investor in the EU, mainly in financial services. In 2017, its share of EU-28 inward FDI stocks reached 35%. Financial services attracted close to three-quarters of total FDI in 2016 (Figure 4.11).

EU-28 has also been a major contributor of FDI to other countries, for which finance and insurance activities also dominated. Finance and insurance activities accounted for 40% of the total outward FDI (Figure 4.12).

Latin America

According to the 2019 World Investment Report, inward FDI flows to Latin America dropped by 5.6% to US$146.7 billion.* The FDI net inflows as a

---

* These findings differ from that presented by the Economic Commission on Latin America and the Caribbean (ECLAC) in a 2019 report, titled Foreign Direct Investment in Latin America and the Caribbean. ECLAC shows that FDI to the region increased by 13.2% due to increased FDI to Brazil and Mexico. The discrepancy in the data stems from the different methods used (for details on the different methodologies, see ECLAC 2019, 28).

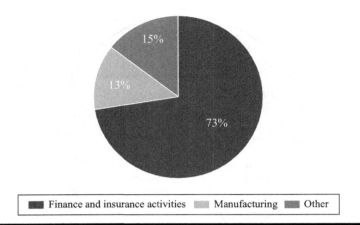

Figure 4.11   Europe FDI inward. Source: Eurostat

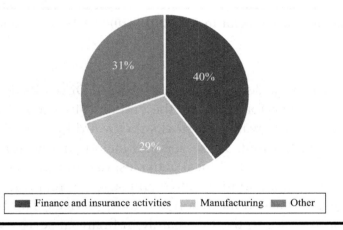

Figure 4.12   Europe FDI outward. Source: Eurostat

percentage of GDP for the region increased from 3.08% in 2017 to 3.4% in 2018. Although FDI inflows declined, FDI inward stocks showed a slight increase from US$2.0 trillion to US$2.1 trillion and represented 40.6% of the GDP. From 2010 to 2019, the Central American country of Panama, unlike other countries in the region, experienced increased investment. This growing level of FDI inflows can be attributed to Panama's development as a logistics and transport hub, as well as its emphasis on securing investment in its services sector.

Most of the region's investment comes from Europe, which provides capital mainly to the Southern Cone, and the United States, which invests predominantly in Mexico and Central America (ECLAC 2019). China also has a strong investment record throughout Latin America, particularly in Brazil. China's investments in the region consist mainly of energy projects. Europe and the United States, on the other hand, engage in a wider variety of investments, which also include mergers and acquisitions in services-based, high-tech industries such as internet and telecommunications (ECLAC 2019). Services received 35% equity compared to 47% for manufactures and 17% for natural resources (ECLAC 2019). The services sector saw a 31% decline in FDI (Sonneland 2018). However, the fastest growing services had ties to the larger digital economy, which includes the rise of software and computer services. Also, the internet, engineering, and construction services saw significant growth (ECLAC 2019, 36).

Intraregional investments have grown in importance, as well, especially in the South American country of Colombia and throughout the Central American subregion (ECLAC 2019). As far as FDI outflows goes, Mexico is the top resource for FDI to the Latin American and Caribbean region at US$6.9 billion (UNCTAD 2019c).

Outward FDI flows and stocks also experienced a decline by 2018 (UNCTAD 2019c, ECLAC 2019). According to the 2019 World Investment Report, the reduction in outward FDI can be attributed to Brazilian foreign affiliates returning financial resources back to their parent companies. Furthermore, Chilean overseas investments decreased.

North America

According to the OECD, the United States has attracted the most FDI inflows for services with US$81 billion. However, the United States trails Canada in terms of FDI stocks in services with 54.1% and 53.3%, respectively.

Canada's manufacturing sector attracts most of the country's FDI inflows at US$202 billion. Nevertheless, several services-based industries were also among the top 10 industries to receive FDI inflows. Some of those industries include management of companies and enterprises with a value of US$175 billion; finance and insurance, US$135 billion; and wholesale trade, US$78 billion.

Mexico's top source of FDI inflows is the United States at 38.8%, according to a Santander Trade report (*Mexico: Foreign Investment* 2020). In 2018, Spain and Canada followed with 13.1% and 10.1%, respectively. Mexico's total FDI reached US$31.6 billion in 2018 (*Mexico: Foreign Investment* 2020). FDI into Mexico's services sector went from US$9.81 billion in 2016 to US$11.95 billion in 2018.

The Mexican financial services industry is the third industry recipient of FDI inflows at 7.9%. Manufacturing, especially automobile manufacturing, receives the most FDI inflows at 49.1%, followed by retail and wholesale trade, 8.9% (*Mexico: Foreign Investment* 2020). The Mexican government under former President Enrique Peña Nieto instituted significant historical reforms to the Mexican telecommunications sector, which has attracted a significant amount of foreign investment. There are opportunities in the financial and insurance services industries as the banking sector continues to grow at a quicker pace (*Mexico: Foreign Investment* 2020).

Numerous opportunities exist for investing in the services sector in the United States. According to the IBIS World Industry Insider, the U.S. services sector reached a value of US$13.9 trillion and 20.5 million service providers in 2013. The top-performing service industries include consulting, housing, healthcare, business support, and consumer goods. IBIS World describes these services as being "among the cream of the crop in the United States economy." At the time of the IBIS report, it was predicted that the industry would grow 7% within a five-year period. Select USA, a Washington, DC-based intergovernmental organization that facilitates investment in the United States, points to the U.S. financial services industry as a significant investment opportunity because of the industry's creative and competitive nature.

"Healthy returns can spur investment," writes industry analyst Ediz Ozelkan (2019) in his study of Canada. Companies that turn a substantial amount of profit present opportunities for investors in the Canadian market. The top three profitable services-based industries in Canada in 2019 are healthcare, real estate, and commercial banking (Ozelkan 2019).

When it comes to investment opportunities in Mexico, financial and insurance services are listed among the significant sectors for the economy. The high potential sectors for investment opportunities in Mexico include a variety of services such as those related to automotive repair, maintenance, etc.; professional and technical services; the banking industry; hotel; and transport (*Mexico: Foreign Investment* 2020).

Middle East*

Unlike the other regions, MENA has experienced a consistent decline in FDI. FDI inflows in the MENA region dropped by more than 50% from

---

* Data on FDI into and out of the Middle East focus on the Middle East and North African (MENA) region, which is included in this section. The often discussed MENA region is due to the fact that the Northern African region's culture and language closely resembles that of the Middle East.

2007 to 2017. In 2007, FDI inflows reached US$80.3 billion before peaking at US$88.5 million a year later. FDI began to show a downward trend following the global economic and financial crisis and political instability throughout the region (*Recent FDI Trends in the MENA Region* 2014). FDI inflows only reached US$28.7 billion by 2017.

Data on FDI toward the services sector in the Middle East alone do not appear to be readily available. However, information is available for those Middle Eastern countries that are also OECD member countries, which are Israel and Turkey. Inward FDI flows for the services sector in Israel increased from US$12 billion in 2017 to US$15 billion in 2018. FDI stocks in services for Israel represented close to 62% of FDI compared to 26% for manufacturing, which also shows the significance of the services sector for economic growth. FDI stock was valued at US$89.6 billion in 2018. Turkey, on the other hand, experienced a decline from around US$5 billion to US$4 billion during the same period. FDI stocks in services for Turkey show a higher portion of 66% of total FDI going toward services and 26%, manufacturing in 2018. FDI stock in services for Turkey was valued at US$97.6 billion in 2018, according to OECD statistics.

Although it only represented 1% of total investment in 2017, Chinese investment in Israel had shown significant growth, particularly in software, IT services, and consumer electronics (*Israel: Foreign Investment* 2020). Investment opportunities in Israel can be found in the following industries: high-tech, aeronautics, and telecommunications (*Israel: Foreign Investment* 2020).

The main investor in the Turkish economy by the first quarter of 2019 was Azerbaijan at 30.3% (*Turkey: Foreign Investment* 2020). Much of this investment goes toward the retail and wholesale, energy, and the financial and insurance services. Numerous opportunities exist for investment in the services sector such as tourism, logistics, transport, and insurance (*Israel: Foreign Investment* 2020).

FDI in the Services Sector and Economic Impact

FDI in the services sector has shown positive gains in some countries and regions while exhibiting mixed results in others. China began liberalizing its services sector, during the early part of the 21st century upon its accession to the World Trade Organization (WTO) on December 11, 2001. For example, for financial services, China's open (0) versus closed (1) ranking dropped from 0.683 in 2003 to 0.540 in 2010, per the OECD FDI restrictiveness index. When it comes to FDI in China's business services sector, the country's OECD restrictiveness ranking dropped from 0.450 in 2003 to 0.338 in 2010. As a result of its more liberal economic approach, FDI to the services sector overall grew threefold from 2000 to 2009 (World Bank 2010). China continued to liberalize its services sector over the last decade. In 2018, China's FDI restrictiveness score, per the same OECD index, was even lower at 0.268 for financial services and 0.225, business services. As a result, China experienced economic growth and development (World Bank 2010). China's significant growth is evident by the fact that it surpassed Japan to become the second largest economy behind the United States in 2010, thus resulting in Japan relinquishing its 42-year hold as the second largest economy.

Productivity growth for interconnected manufacturing-based industries has also been a by-product of FDI in services in developing countries such as Chile. Since Chile received significant amounts of FDI in its services sector in the 1990s, it can also have a positive effect on the productivity growth of the manufacturing plants that maximize the use of certain services (see Fernandes and Paunov 2008). Intra-European FDI in Europe has led to the creation of new jobs, economic growth, and productivity gains for local firms in the host regions (Sunesen et al. 2018).

The global health pandemic of 2020 has had a negative impact on the FDI to the emerging and developing economies. These economies still rely mainly on FDI in the agricultural and manufacturing sector. Due to the reduction in FDI in these areas and the significant contraction of activity, the emerging and developing economies are impacted negatively. On the other hand, the services sector remains an important part of developed economies. The increase in earnings that can be reinvested in the healthcare, technology, and communication sectors prove beneficial in the developed economies.

Discussion for Businesses and Policymakers

Countries that liberalize their investment market and create competition with a strong institutional framework will attract FDI, including to the services sector. This, in turn, leads to positive gains for an economy and presents opportunities for investors overseas. However, the realities must be taken into account. "Digital services depend on infrastructure for delivery, and without digital services, infrastructure providers have little for their infrastructure to do" (World Economic Forum 2014). Digital infrastructure refers to mobile and internet services, digital ID, and electricity. The expansion of cross-border services through the use of digital technology creates a number of opportunities for businesses, employees, and consumers.

> By creating digital market institutions and values ... digital platforms can reduce transaction costs compared to the analog world, thus creating opportunities, especially for micro, small, and medium enterprises (MSMEs) in domestic and foreign markets. They may open up new markets, lower the barriers to entrepreneurship, bring in non-professionals and peers, and provide new sources of finance to small-scale start-ups.
> For individuals, digital platforms allow access to more variety and choice of goods and services at lower costs ... Moreover, in terms of employment, an expanding digital economy in developing countries can generate new high-skilled jobs, especially in the core digital sector and in areas requiring relatively advanced technical and analytical skills.
>
> **(UNCTAD 2019a, 34)**

Even with the FDI in the digital sector via projects, the reality when it comes to the services sector is that 50% of the world's population remains offline, only 20% of the population in least developed countries (LDCs) are online compared to 80% in developed countries (UNCTAD 2019a, 13). Furthermore, there remains a gender gap in which women and girls often lack access to the internet compared to men and boys (OECD 2018a; UNCTAD 2019a). Globally, that gap increased slightly in 2017 compared to 2013. The widest gap in male and female penetration rates or internet usage exists in the LDCs at 32.9% and sub-Saharan Africa at 25.3%, where the gap has increased from 2013 to 2017 (UNCTAD 2019a, 14). The gender gap in internet usage in developed countries decreased during the same four-year time frame and reached 2.8% (UNCTAD 2019a, 14). The disparities in access to digital technology, which allows for the continued provision of services across borders, result in a large segment of the global population lacking access to the benefits from the digital economy.

Such a reality presents an opportunity for collaboration between the public and private sectors to develop an FDI strategy that invests in developing the infrastructure that supports the use of digital services. Investing in infrastructure in this context refers to capital and a well-thought-out, effective strategy beyond the digital technology and services themselves toward those services industries that are also impacted by digital technology. One such services-based industry that is also essential is in the area of education. Whereas many educational services are able to extend beyond national borders quickly and at a lower cost due to availability of digital services, not everyone can enjoy the benefits of such services in both developed and developing countries, although the lack of access is much higher in the latter.

The increased provision of medical and healthcare services through virtual means via a personal computer, smartphone, or tablet helped to reduce the traditional in-person doctor visits as a way to keep patients safe during the COVID-19 pandemic. As quickly as healthcare services shifted, so did the deeper revelation of the gap between those with adequate technological access and those without.

The same results emerged in the digital financial services sector. The digital financial services sector has played a role in boosting inclusion in the financial economy. More specifically, small business owners and citizens along the lower-income spectrum could gain access to capital, buy and sell goods, and receive payment through services provided digitally, which was often a challenge through traditional financial institutions. The same challenges with poor digital infrastructure inhibit the ability for the financial services that rely on digital technology to reach its maximum potential in terms of financial inclusion, per observations by the International Monetary Fund (IMF) (von Allmen et al 2020).

Investment in building strong Wi-Fi networks across a variety of geographical regions (urban and rural), programs that boost the number of people who have access to computers, and developing the skills of primary, secondary, and postsecondary students; entrepreneurs; consumers from diverse backgrounds, etc. to be able to leverage the services offered in the digital economy. Additionally, investment in efforts to ensure that everyone has access to basic things such as electricity and batteries must also be considered to deepen the inclusion rates in the digital economy.

Bibliography

Administrator. 2013. "Top performing service industries."*IBIS World database*, Retrieved June 24, 2020. https://www.ibisworld.com/industry-insider/analyst -insights/top-performing-service-industries/.

Bureau of Economic Analysis. 2019. *New Foreign Direct Investment in the United States, 2018.* Suitland, MD: Bureau of Economic Analysis.

2019. "ASEAN investment report 2019 FDI in services: Focus on health care." In ASEAN Investment Report *2019 FDI in Services: Focus on Health Care.* Jakarta: ASEAN. https://asean.org/asean-investment-report-2019-fdi-services-focus-health-care/.

Chakraborty, Subhayan. 2020. Inbound FDI rose 14% in FY20 to $49.9 Billion; service sector top recipient. *Business Standard.* Accessed August 28, 2020. https://www.business-standard.com/article/economy-policy/inbound-fdi-rose-14-in-fy20-to-49-9-billion-service-sector-top-recipient-120052801467_1.html.

Dettoni, Jacopo. 2020. "Which FDI sectors could benefit from the coronavirus crisis?" *FDI Intelligence.* Accessed May 20, 2020. https://www.fdiintelligence.com/article/77085.

Economic Commission for Latin America and the Caribbean. 2019. *Foreign Direct Investment in Latin America and the Caribbean (ECLAC).* Santiago: ECLAC.

Eriksson von Allmen; Ulric, Purva Khera; Sumiko Ogawa; and Ratna Sahay. 2020. "Digital financial inclusion in the times of COVID-19." July 1. https://blogs.imf.org/2020/07/01/digital-financial-inclusion-in-the-times-of-covid-19/.

Eurostat. 2019. *Foreign Direct Investment: Stocks.* https://ec.europa.eu/eurostat/statistics-explained/index.php/Foreign_direct_investment_-_stocks.

EY. 2018. "Turning tides EY's attractiveness program." Accessed May 24, 2020. https://assets.ey.com/content/dam/ey-sites/ey-com/en_za/topics/attractiveness/ey-turning-tides-2018.pdf.

Fernandes, Ana M. 2007. *Structure and Performance of the Services Sector in Transition Economies. edited by Development Research Group and Trade Team.* Washington, DC: World Bank.

Fernandes, Ana M.; and Caroline Paunov. 2008. Foreign direct investment in services and manufacturing productivity growth: Evidence for Chile. In *Evidence for Chile,* edited by Development Research Group Trade Team. Washington, DC: World Bank.

Hoekman, Bernard. 2018. "Trade in Services: Opening Markets to Create Opportunities." In *Industries Without Smokestacks: Industrialization in Africa Reconsidered* edited by Richard Newfarmer, John Page and Finn Tarp, 151–169. Oxford, UK: Oxford University Press.

"Israel: Foreign investment." 2020. *Santander Trade.* Accessed August 22, 2020. https://santandertrade.com/en/portal/establish-overseas/israel/foreign-investment.

Keelery, Sandhya. 2020. "FDI equity inflows distribution India FY 2020 by sector." Statista. Accessed August 15, 2020. https://www.statista.com/statistics/711398/india-fdi-equity-inflows-distribution-by-sector/.

Kirkegaard, Jacob Funk. 2012. Transactions: A New Look at Service Sector Foreign Direct Investment in Asia. In *Asian Development Bank.* Manila, Philippines: Asian Development Bank.

Madden, Payce. 2019. "Figure of the week: Foreign direct investment in Africa." *Africa in Focus.* https://www.brookings.edu/blog/africa-in-focus/2019/10/09/figure-of-the-week-foreign-direct-investment-in-africa/.

Maister, Philippa. 2020. What will digitisation mean for FDI? *FDI Intelligence.* Accessed August 16, 2020.

Mazachek, Kara. 2020. "Global Outlook: United States Remains the Largest Destination for FDI in the World." March 17. https://blog.trade.gov/2020/03/17/global-outlook-united-states-remains-the-largest-destination-for-fdi-in-the-world/.

McPhillips, Deidre. 2019. 10 Countries That Receive the Most Foreign Direct Investment. US News and World Report.

"Mexico: Foreign Investment." 2020. Santander Trade. Accessed August 22, 2020. https://santandertrade.com/en/portal/establish-overseas/mexico/foreign-investment.

Newfarmer, Richard; John Page; and Finn Tarp. 2018. "Industries without smokestacks and structural transformation in Africa: Overview." In *Industries without Smokestacks: Industrialization in Africa Reconsidered*, 1–26. Oxford, UK: Oxford University Press.

OECD (Organization for Economic Cooperation and Development). 2014. "Draft background note: Recent FDI trends in the MENA region." In LAS-OECD Regional Conference and MENA-OECD Regional Investment Working Group, Cairo, Egypt.

OECD. 2018a. *Bridging the Digital Gender Divide: Include, Upskill, Innovate.* Paris, France: OECD.

OECD. 2018b. "Global investment grows America's economy." In *Foreign Direct Investment in the United States 2018*. Washington, DC: Organization for International Investment.

OECD. n.d. Globalisation: FDI and multinational enterprises. In OECD Factbook 2010. Paris, France: OECD.

OECD. 2020. Outward FDI stocks by partner country (indicator). doi: 10.1787/b550f49f-en (Accessed on June 1, 2020)

OFII (Organization for International Investment). 2018. *Foreign Direct Investment in the United States.* Washington, DC: Organization for International Investment.

Ozelkan, Ediz. 2019. "Top 10 Canadian Industries by Profit Margin." Retrieved July 6, 2020 from IBIS World database. https://www.ibisworld.com/industry-insider/analyst-insights/top-10-canadian-industries-by-profit-margin/.

Select USA. 2020. "Financial Services Spotlight." International Trade Administration, U.S. Department of Commerce. Accessed August 28. https://www.selectusa.gov/financial-services-industry-united-states.

Seric, Adnan; and Jostein Hauge. 2020. "Foreign direct investments could contract by 40% this year, hitting developing countries hardest." June 2. https://www.weforum.org/agenda/2020/06/coronavirus-covid19-economics-fdi-investment-united-nations/.

Sharma, Samrat. 2020. "FDI into India may go into freefall in 2020; here's what to hit foreign investment inflows." Financial Express. Accessed August 16. https://www.financialexpress.com/economy/fdi-into-india-may-go-into-freefall-in-2020-heres-what-to-hit-foreign-investment-inflows/1994180/.

Sonneland, Holly K. 2018. "Chart: FDI in Latin America and the Caribbean." *Americas Society/Council of the Americas*. Accessed June 6, 2020. https://www.as-coa.org/articles/chart-fdi-latin-america-and-caribbean.

"South Africa: Foreign investment." *Santander Trade*. Accessed August 22, 2020. https://santandertrade.com/en/portal/establish-overseas/south-africa/foreign-investment.

Spray, John; and Sebastian Wolf. 2018. "Industries without smokestacks in Uganda and Rwanda." In *Industries without Smokestacks: Industrialization in Africa Reconsidered*, edited by Richard Newfarmer, John Page and Finn Tarp, 341–363. Oxford, UK: Oxford University Press.

Sunesen, Eva Rytter; Tine Jeppesen; Jonas Juul Henriksen; and Julien Grunfelder. 2018. *The World in Europe: Global FDI Flows towards Europe*. Brussels, Belgium: ESPON.

"Turkey: Foreign investment." *Santander Trade*, Last Modified June 20, 2020. Accessed June 25, 2020.

UNCTAD (United Nations Conference on Trade and Development). 2019a. *Digital Economy Report: Value Creation and Capture: Implications for Developing Countries*. New York, NY: UNCTAD.

UNCTAD. 2019b. Foreign Direct Investment to Africa Defies Global Slump, Rises 11%. Accessed August 20, 2020. https://unctad.org/news/foreign-direct-investment-africa-defies-global-slump-rises-11.

UNCTAD. 2019c. World Investment Report 2019: Special Economic Zones. In World Investment Report *2019*. New York, NY: UNCTAD.

UNCTAD. 2020a. *Global FDI Flows Flat in 2019 Moderate Increase Expected in 2020*. New York, NY: UNCTAD.

UNCTAD. 2020b. "Global investment flows flat in 2019, moderate increase expected in 2020." Accessed August 14. https://unctad.org/en/pages/newsdetails.aspx?OriginalVersionID=2274.

UNCTAD. 2020c. *Investment Trends Monitor: Impact of the Coronavirus Outbreak on Global FDI*. New York, NY: UNCTAD.

World Bank. 2010. *Foreign Direct Investment: The China Story*. Washington, DC: World Bank.

World Economic Forum. April 2014. "Introduction: The digital infrastructure imperative." In *Delivering Digital Infrastructure: Advancing the Internet Economy*. Geneva: World Economic Forum.

GUIDE TO EXPORTING A SERVICE

Chapter 5

Identifying Market Opportunities

The national-level reforms that many countries have undertaken to integrate into the global economy and become more interconnected have led to the increased trade and foreign direct investment flows highlighted in the previous section. The services sector continues to play a significant role in connecting the global economy. However, based on observations in the United States, many government-sponsored export workshops, discussions, training sessions, and seminars still focus heavily on trade in manufactured goods and agricultural commodities. Consequently, service providers receive minimal information and training on how to leverage their competitive advantage and identify the opportunities internationally. This chapter fills in that gap by detailing the global market opportunities for service providers that will save them both time and money. The opportunities that reduce the amount of resources that would be expended trying to go it alone are presented by two key mechanisms: 1) reciprocal trade agreements and 2) projects funded by international financial institutions or multilateral development banks.

Opportunity #1: Reciprocal Trade Agreements and Ease of Access

Many business owners and executives have heard of trade agreements. At the same time, few fully understand trade agreements. To fully grasp the opportunities presented by trade agreements, it is important to comprehend their different types. Reciprocal trade agreements (RTAs) refer to those trade deals in which all member countries benefit from preferential access to each other's markets. That preferential access comes in the form of reduced or eliminated tariffs for goods and fewer technical or regulatory barriers to trade for goods and services.

The RTAs can be structured as a bilateral agreement between two countries such as the U.S.-Chile trade deal and the Mexico–Japan trade agreement. RTAs may also include countries from the same region such as the United States-Mexico-Canada Agreement (USMCA), Association of Southeast Asian Nations (ASEAN), the Southern Common Market (Mercosur), the African Continental Free Trade Area (AfCFTA), and the European Free Trade Association (EFTA). There are also cross-regional RTAs, as in the case of the Comprehensive and Progressive Agreements for Trans-Pacific Partnership (CPTPP) and the Central America-Dominican Republic-United States Free Trade Agreement (CAFTA-DR). Additionally, multilateral trade agreements refer to the trade rules that apply to a larger group of countries from all around the world. The General Agreement on Tariffs and Trade (GATT) and the General Agreement on Trade in Services (GATS) exemplify multilateral trade agreements (Table 5.1).

Reciprocal trade agreements differ from unilateral trade programs, which offer one-way preferential access. In other words, in a trade relationship between two parties, only one party would enjoy preferential access to other party's market. Several unilateral trade programs that provide preferential access to agricultural and goods producers from developing countries to the United States. The Generalized System of Preferences (GSP) was established by the Trade Act of 1974 eliminated tariffs on select products from 119

Table 5.1   Types and Examples of Reciprocal Trade Agreements Signed by the United States

Bilateral	Regional	Cross-regional	Multilateral
Australia Bahrain Chile Colombia Israel Jordan Morocco South Korea Panama Peru Singapore	North America: U.S.-Mexico-Canada (USMCA)	Central America-Dominican Republic Free Trade Agreement (CAFTA-DR)	General Agreement on Tariffs and Trade (GATT) General Agreement on Trade in Services (GATS)

designated beneficiary countries and territories to promote economic growth and development in developing countries. The United States established similar unilateral trade programs for different regions such as the Caribbean Basin Initiative/Caribbean Basin Trade Partnership Act (CBI/CBTPA) in 1983 and 2000 and the African Growth and Opportunities Act (AGOA) in 2000. Services exports are not included in any of these unilateral programs.

In addition to the lack of full understanding of trade agreements, several businesses that could benefit from these trade deals do not use them. A 2015 Thomson Reuters and KPMG survey revealed that most companies that import and/or export do not use the trade agreements that are available to them. Some reasons for not taking advantage of this opportunity include the lack of time and resources, inability to adequately understand the cross-border rules, and failure to integrate technology into their processes and procedures.

In January 2020, the UK Trade Policy Observatory (UKTPO), which studies small and medium-sized enterprises (SMEs) in the European Union, reported that, although the general provisions in trade agreements may reduce trade barriers, they may also increase the costs for the SMEs. Whereas larger firms may still be able to expand successfully, these trade barriers disproportionately affect the SMEs (USITC 2010). The same survey revealed that only 19% of exporters used trade agreements to sell their goods and services beyond the EU. Fifty-two percent of EU-based SMEs reported not using trade deals. The remaining 29% of respondents did not know if they were using trade deals. The SMEs in the European Union that considered using trade agreements weighed the costs and benefits of using a trade agreement versus the administrative costs associated with comprehending the trade agreement provisions and how to leverage them. The costs of the latter outweighed the former for these SMEs. Although the SMEs may find trade agreements costly, not using them leads to costs created by technical barriers to trade, restricted access, and the lack of protection against discriminatory and unfair trade practices.

Having insight into the structure of a reciprocal agreement also helps to comprehend the opportunities that they present to service providers. Reciprocal trade agreements similarly include chapters pertaining to market access for goods, services, foreign investment, intellectual property, among other important areas in cross-border trade. The chapters that impact service providers as they export to other countries are those pertaining to services, investment, government procurement, and intellectual property (Figure 5.1).

National treatment is among the specific provisions that allow for preferential access in the cross-border trade of services. National treatment

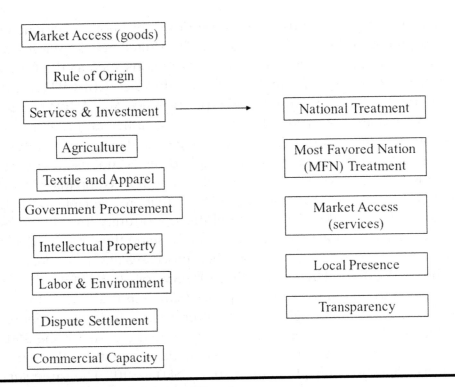

Figure 5.1   General Trade Agreement Structure

prohibits any member territory from not allowing for services to be provided by a company from another member territory on the basis that it is a foreign service provider. Most-Favoured-Nation Treatment (MFN) restricts any treatment that is not the same as that offered to service providers from other member territories. Market access refers to the access to other markets through the reduction or elimination of regulatory barriers to trade. Local presence says that the member countries cannot require that a service provider from another member country to set up an office or affiliate, or to be a resident, in its country or territory in order to provide the service. The rule regarding transparency maintains that the policies and regulations should be communicated clearly among the trading partners.

United States-Mexico-Canada Agreement

As a trade agreement that took effect in 2020, the USMCA exemplifies the opportunities presented by a regional trade deal. The USMCA was signed by all three countries in 2018 and took effect on July 1, 2020. The USMCA replaced the 26-year-old North American Free Trade Agreement (NAFTA).

Furthermore, the USMCA advances the opportunities in the cross-border trade in services due to its provisions addressing the ever-growing digital economy in the 21st century. Digital technology enhances the ability for services to bypass borders and reach citizens all around the world at an even faster pace and at a lower cost.

Chapter 15 of the USMCA focuses on the cross-border trade in services. The services included in this chapter include professional services, which are defined as one "which requires specialized post-secondary education, or equivalent training or experience, and for which the right to practice is granted or restricted by a Party..." (USMCA Chapter 15). (Financial services, air services, and those services provided by government-backed programs are addressed in separate chapters within the USMCA.)

The chapter lays out the rules as they pertain to national treatment, which was also a part of NAFTA. A service provider from the United States should receive the same treatment as a local service provider in Canada or Mexico and vice-versa. Should any such illegal trade practices take place, business owners and executives can seek consultations with the appropriate agencies and/or use the dispute settlement mechanism outlined in Chapter 31. The dispute settlement process is designed to resolve trade disputes, in which one trade partner alleges that another partner engages in trade practices that violate the terms of the USMCA.

Resources exist to help service providers further understand and navigate the USMCA. For instance, the U.S. Customs and Border Protection (CBP) opened the USMCA Center in Washington, D.C. (While NAFTA was in effect, the Office of NAFTA assisted businesses with any inquiries regarding its implementation.)

Chapter 15 also includes an article regarding the MFN treatment. Goods and services traded among the USMCA member countries must receive treatment that is no less favorable than that offered to other non-member countries, according to the MFN rule.

Article 15.5 offers details on market access in general. Service providers from any of the three USMCA member countries should not face any restrictions, such as quotas, economic needs tests, or legal entity requirements, on their ability to access to another member country's market.

The following article, Article 15.6, is titled "Local Presence," which states:

> No party shall require a service supplier of another Party to establish or maintain a representative office or an enterprise, or to be resident, in its territory as a condition for the cross-border supply

of a service.... Subparagraph (a) (iii) does not cover measures of a Party which limit inputs for the supply of services.

In other words, the USMCA prohibits the requirement by any member country that a foreign service provider set up an office in its country in order to provide a service in that same country. The *local presence* article opens the opportunity for North American service providers to access markets within the region much more easily and without the costs associated with establishing another office.

Chapter 17 includes rules as they pertain to the cross-border trade of financial services. Each member country continues to uphold its commitment to liberalize trade in financial services. In other words, financial services can be provided by any of the North American countries without facing trade barriers by another member. The USMCA has modernized the NAFTA agreement to meet the needs of digital services as they apply to the financial services industry. For instance, the USMCA prohibits any requirement for local data storage. Rather, the agreement allows for the cross-border transfer of data and encourages transparency when it comes to regulations, licensing practices and other authorizations as they pertain to market access. U.S. financial services exports to Canada and Mexico reached US$8.4 billion in 2017, according to data collected from the International Trade Centre. The United States imported US$4.4 billion worth of financial services from Canada in 2017.* Canada's financial services exports to Mexico reached US$30.8 million, and it imported US$24.7 million worth of the same service from Mexico in 2017 (Trade Map). The Office of United States Trade Representative (USTR) indicated that "[b]y further levelling the playing field, it is anticipated that the USMCA will grant the United States wider market access to financial service firms that are operating in each other's countries" ("United States-Mexico-Canada Trade Fact Sheet"). In other words, financial services trade throughout North America has the potential to increase with the USMCA.

Chapter 19 of the USMCA focuses solely on digital trade, which makes the USMCA the first comprehensive agreement to include in-depth provisions regarding digital trade. The chapter prohibits the application of customs duties toward any products distributed electronically such as e-books, videos, music, software, and games. Additionally, limits cannot be placed on any data that has been stored and transferred across borders. The provision

---

* Information on Mexico's exports of financial services to the United States are not available.

ensures consumer protection, multimember collaboration toward cyberse-curity, and limiting the liability of any third-party internet platform, except when it comes to IP enforcement. The chapter's provisions on digital trade present opportunities for service providers that also rely on digital technology to access any of the three markets much easier and have resources through the dispute settlement process should there be a violation of the agreement.

Chapter 20 touches on the issue of intellectual property. The USMCA encourages the same treatment in terms of copyright, trademark, and patent protection for both domestic and foreign creators. The USMCA strengthens the intellectual property chapter of NAFTA by requiring that IP enforcement procedures and proper penalties exist for any IP violations. The benefit to the service providers is that there are protections and enforcement that allows for continued innovation and growth. Without such protections, companies find themselves paying the costs associated with the loss of IP, fraud, and the lack of recourse should there be a violation of IP rights.

The USMCA advances the provisions within NAFTA by focusing on small businesses. When NAFTA took effect, much focus remained on the role of large multinational corporations (MNCs) and big businesses on the terms of the deal (Lewis and Ebrahim 1993). At the same time, Christensen (1993) questioned whether there was a role for small businesses with NAFTA and concluded in the affirmative, since the deal would reduce the costs of export through the removal of many trade barriers. Nevertheless, many argued that small businesses did not carry as much influence on the NAFTA talks as the larger MNCs.

The same discussion about the minimal role and influence that small businesses played on the final results of an agreement entered into discussions surrounding the Trans-Pacific Partnership (TPP) agreement. The TPP included all three USMCA countries and served as the basis for some of the provisions within the final agreement between the three North American countries. (The TPP was supposed to create a trade bloc of 12 countries throughout the Asia-Pacific region, which, combined, accounted for 40% of world trade and a GDP in 2017 of US$27.4 trillion.*) Although the TPP included strong provisions in the areas in services and investment and would have given U.S. exporters access to five additional markets—Brunei Darussalam, Japan, Malaysia, New Zealand, Vietnam—many small

---

* The TPP countries included Australia, Brunei Darussalam, Canada, Chile, Japan, Malaysia, Mexico, New Zealand, Peru, Singapore, the United States, and Vietnam.

businesses were opposed to the agreement for various reasons (Acharya 2015; Marks 2016). One reason that resonated loudly was the lack of transparency throughout the process. For instance, a 2015 editorial in the *Maine Beacon* newspaper states:

> The TPP is designed to deliberately remove many layers of democracy, public input, and scrutiny in decision-making. This is a net loss for democracy at every level. The TPP replaces democracy with private, corporate power over many economic decision....
>
> The aims of the TPP are contrary to the interests of small, local businesses in Maine. The TPP will not strengthen our local economies.... It will not allow greater access to locally produced goods and services.
>
> The TPP favors a handful of large multinational corporate entities, and it destroys the checks and balances that allow smaller businesses to succeed (Jackimovicz 2015).

In the end, all countries signed the agreement on February 4, 2016 in New Zealand, but the United States withdrew from the trade deal on January 23, 2017. As a result, the remaining 11 TPP member countries moved forward with a revised deal, the Comprehensive and Progressive Agreement for Trans-Pacific Partnership (CPTPP), the following year.

The original TPP included a chapter specifically for small and medium-sized enterprises—Chapter 24—which included three articles. Article 24.1 of the TPP stated that "[e]ach Party shall establish or maintain its own publicly accessible website containing information regarding this Agreement...." Article 24.2 creates a Committee on SMEs, and Articles 24.3 indicates that the dispute settlement provisions in Chapter 28 will not apply to any matters arising from the key points in Chapter 24. Although the United States is no longer a part of the TPP, the same effort to include provisions specifically for SMEs was successfully put toward the USMCA.

Within the USMCA, Chapter 25 focuses on SMEs and goes further than the provisions that were in the TPP agreement. The member countries recognize "the fundamental role of SMEs in maintaining dynamism and enhancing competitiveness of their respective economies" and "shall foster close cooperation between SMEs of the Parties and cooperate in promoting jobs and growth in SMEs" (Article 25.1). The remaining specific articles within the SME chapter address the following matters:

- Cooperation among the member countries to boost trade and investment opportunities for SMEs;
- Sharing of information via a website that is accessible publicly;
- Establishing the SME Committee, which consists of government representatives from each country to promote opportunities for SMEs;
- Incorporating dialogue between the SME Committee and other stakeholders such as the private sector, employees, non-government organizations, academicians, and business-owners from diverse background and underrepresented groups; and
- Recognizing the advantages to SMEs that are also offered under other chapters (e.g. cross-border trade in services and digital trade).

The final article, similar to that of the TPP, does not allow for the use of the dispute settlement mechanism under Chapter 25. "No Party shall have recourse to dispute settlement under Chapter 31 (Dispute Settlement) for any matter arising under this chapter" (USMCA Article 25.7). This chapter presents increased opportunities for SMEs to participate in discussions surrounding the USMCA to ensure the benefit of the various chapters and specific provisions for SMEs.

Service providers may face higher costs in those countries with which its home country has not signed and implemented a trade agreement. For instance, U.S. service providers to the Chinese market have faced huge costs in this market. China is a large potential market, with 1.4 billion citizens, for U.S. services exports, which have increased ten-fold from a little under US$6 billion in 2003 to US$60 billion a year. Despite the huge market potential, U.S. services exports to China pale in comparison to these same exports to other parts of the world (Zumbrun 2019). That is due to the non-tariff barriers that hinder the ability of U.S. companies to expand and compete in the Chinese market. Some of these barriers come from China's laws pertaining to cybersecurity, healthcare, and financial services that increase the costs of doing business in China (AmCham Shanghai 2018). Unlike the provisions in the USMCA, China requires that foreign companies store their data locally. Furthermore, many service providers must become a part of a joint venture and maintain a minority controlling share in the ICT sector and a cap at 70% for the healthcare industry (AmCham Shanghai 2018). These restrictions in the services sector have also cost companies competitiveness in the Chinese market. For example, credit card operators continue to push to be able to process payments in China, which has produced minimal success. Social media platform companies, such as YouTube and Facebook, are either completely blocked or face censorship in China.

On the other hand, much of the Chinese population has spent money on U.S. educational and travel services, for which the United States has thought about restricting their use of such services through the visa-system (Zumbrun 2019).

According to a 2017 National Bureau of Asian Research report, titled "The Theft of American Intellectual Property: Reassessments of the Challenge and United States Policy," activities, such as selling counterfeit goods and pirated software and stealing trade secrets by China and other countries, costs the U.S. economy anywhere between US$225 billion and US$600 billion. About 20% of the North American corporations that participated in a CNBC Global CFO Council survey reported that their intellectual property had been stolen by Chinese companies (Rosenbaum 2019). Without a comprehensive trade deal that has been signed and implemented between the United States and China, U.S. service providers will continue to encounter stiff challenges to their ability to leverage any opportunities that may exist in such a large market. For this reason, trade deals present greater opportunities in terms of ease of access, which lowers some of the transaction costs.

Brazil is another large market that attracted the interest of U.S. companies, including SMEs, especially when its economy was considered one of the fastest growing economies in the world. Brazil's annual growth rate reached 4.5% from 2006 to 2010 (World Bank). Regarding U.S.–Brazil trade in services, U.S. services exports to the South American country reached US$24.6 billion, and it reported a US$18 billion surplus in 2019. U.S. services exports increased 81% compared to a decade earlier, according to USTR figures. The key exports from the United States to Brazil have been in travel, transport, telecommunications, computer, and information services, and most of these service-based exports are by U.S.-owned affiliates. However, certain restrictions and legislation in Brazil create a market that is more difficult to access and within which to be competitive, especially since the United States and Brazil have yet to engage in official trade talks, sign, and implement a bilateral trade agreement.

When it comes to the government procurement process, Brazil's Normative Instruction 10/2020 now makes it easier for foreign suppliers of goods and services to bid on a project, which took effect in May 2020. At the same time, Brazil still requires that foreign companies establish a subsidiary, enter into a joint venture, or acquire a partner in some industries such as telecommunications, per the "Brazil – Country Commercial Guide" published by the International Trade Administration.

The key recommendation for companies, especially the SMEs looking to expand, whether they are U.S. firms or companies based in other countries around the world, is to begin with the opportunities presented by a reciprocal trade agreement signed between the home country and other countries.

Other types of agreements between countries exist that offer some level of commitment in the cross-border trade in goods and services, although they are not comprehensive and specific. Countries may sign an agreement that promotes trade and investment between two or more partners. For instance, the United States has only negotiated and signed one reciprocal trade deal with an African country—United States-Morocco Free Trade Agreement. However, the United States has signed trade and investment agreements with a number of other African countries, as in the case of the Trade, Investment, and Development Agreement (TIDCA) with the Southern African Customs Union (SACU), which includes Botswana, Eswatini (formerly Swaziland), Lesotho, Namibia, and South Africa. (The United States has signed 56 Trade and Investment Framework Agreements (TIFAs) with countries all throughout the world, mostly with the African and Middle East regions.) Nevertheless, these TIFAs offer an opportunity for exporting a service in another market, even though they are not as detailed as a reciprocal trade agreement.

Finally, the U.S. bilateral investment treaty (BIT) program helps to protect private investment to develop market-oriented policies in partner countries and to promote U.S. exports. The protocols allow for natural treatment for specific services in the countries with which the United States has a BIT. As in the case of the TIFA, the BITs do not break down the rules as they pertain to services. However, they do create an opening for encouraging fair cross-border trade in services.

The programs which allow for preferential access into each other's markets are a good starting point for service providers when exporting a service. An awareness of such programs helps a business owner or executive identify the market opportunities. Furthermore, having some idea of the rules that pertain to the services sector within trade agreements sheds even more light on the opportunities available (Figure 5.2).

Opportunity #2: Government-Funded Services-Based Projects

Another mechanism that allows for service-providers to enter international markets much easier than going it alone are the number of funded projects

Trade Agreement	Year Signed	National Treatment	MFN Treatment	Market Access	Intellectual Property	E-commerce	Digital Trade
With the United States							
Australia	2004	X	X	X	X	X	
Bahrain	2004	X	X	X	X	X	
Chile	2003	X	X	X	X	X	
Colombia	2006						
Dominican Republic-Central America (DR-CAFTA)	2004	X	X	X	X	X	
Israel	1985	X	X	X	X		
Jordan	2001	X	X	X	X	X	
Morocco	2004	X	X	X	X	X	
Oman	2006	X	X	X	X	X	
Panama	2007	X	X	X	X	X	
Peru	2009	X	X	X	X	X	
Singapore	2003						
South Korea	2007						
USMCA	2018	X	X	X	X	X	X

Figure 5.2   U.S. Trade Deals and Key Areas Covered

and grants that exist. Unfortunately, many companies, especially the SMEs, are either completely unaware of this opportunity; do not know how to navigate the funding process; or do not have the time, human capital, and expertise to apply for these projects quickly and consistently. As a result, these companies miss out on some of the benefits, which may include multiyear funding, billions of dollars' worth of business, a transparent system, and a secure payment process. These opportunities can be found via several organizations, which will be discussed here (see Chapter 7 for a step-by-step process on leveraging such opportunities).

Federal government agencies, as in the case of the United States, offer contracts and/or grants that allow service-based companies to provide a service overseas. Additionally, multilateral development banks or international financial institutions fund a number of development projects globally, many of which request the assistance of service providers.

U.S. Agency for International Development (USAID)

USAID funds projects focused on international economic development and transformative change in countries around the world. These projects can be located on the organization's website at www.usaid.gov. The projects are organized by themes, which include, but are not limited to, the following:

- Agriculture and food security
- Economic growth and trade
- Education
- Gender equality and women's empowerment
- Global health

For those service-providers interested in specific countries or regions, they can also identify projects based on their geographical preference. According to the USAID website, the agency is slated to receive US$19.6 billion in funds budgeted for fiscal year 2021. Some of these projects may align with current policy changes, especially when it comes to the implementation of trade agreements. For instance, all tariffs on U.S.-Dominican agricultural trade will be removed by 2025. USAID has been funding projects that are designed to develop the Dominican agricultural sector so that producers of different commodities can compete once these tariffs are removed completely.

World Bank

The World Bank, an international financial institution that goes as far back as 1944, presents another opportunity for individual firms to export a service overseas in a more open and transparent manner. Projects funded by the World Bank are also organized by countries and themes. Some of the relevant themes include, but are not limited to, economic policy, finance, human development and gender, and private sector development. Projects take place in more than 170 countries around the globe, excluding Andorra, Cuba, Liechenstein, Monaco, and North Korea. In FY2018, the World Bank budgeted US$10 billion on 1,600 projects in 132 countries, in which most of the funds went toward transport followed by water, sanitation, and waste.

International Development Finance Corporation (IDFC)

The Washington, D.C.-based IDFC replaced the long-standing Overseas Private Investment Corporation (OPIC) in December 2019. The IDFC builds upon and expands OPIC's mission to invest in foreign infrastructures, as well as provide aid in the areas of female entrepreneurship, human rights, and labor rights in more than 160 countries around the world. In sum, the goal of the IDFC is to provide solutions to promote development, as well as support U.S. foreign policy and national security objectives.

According to the IDFC website, organizations can begin the investment process through the same site. In 2020, as a response to the global health pandemic caused by COVID-19, the IDFC issued a *Call for Proposal* in the areas of health, as well as information technology and communications, in eligible countries worldwide.

U.S. Department of State

The State Department offers grants to businesses to provide services in overseas markets. The website includes detailed information about the awards process and the awards that are available in a variety of areas such as education and technology. Additionally, the State Department may fund projects that are a collaborative effort with other organizations worldwide. For instance, the *La Idea Incubator Project* is funded by the State Department and emphasizes enhancing entrepreneurship and job creation throughout the Western Hemisphere. Furthermore, the project places a special emphasis on trade promotion between the United States and the Central American region. The project emerges from a collaborative effort between the International Business Innovation Association (INBIA) and the Regional Center for the Promotion of MSMEs (CENPROMYPE).

U.S. Department of Agriculture

The USDA has offices in overseas markets and funds projects on which service providers in the area of agriculture could participate, for example, education on using modern technology and improved farming techniques and practices. The processes and procedures for registering as a vendor and learning about opportunities available for service suppliers are available on the USDA's website under the Office of Contracting and Procurement.

U.S. Department of Defense

The U.S. Department of Defense funds projects pertaining to the military. There are projects for consultants on military strategy, etc.

U.S. Department of Education

Finally, the U.S. Department of Education also funds projects around the globe. These educational projects seek to improve school infrastructure, learning systems, as well as increase access to reduce inequalities around the globe.

This is not an exhaustive list of all government agencies. Nevertheless, the point is to show how a service supplier can go after grants and contracts that would allow them to provide a service overseas.

In addition to the World Bank, there are multilateral development banks (MDBs) at the regional level that present opportunities for companies. The key thing to keep in mind is that each agency may have its own unique process, which one should understand. Nevertheless, the general description of the MDBs is provided here, for which the World Bank does have a commercial advisor involved with each. The Inter-American Development Bank (IDB) offers a number of projects to its 26 borrowing member countries, all of which are in Latin America and the Caribbean.* However, the IDB has a total of 48 member countries. The IDB lends out US$12.7 billion each year. The main client base for the IDB are the governments for which there is a standard pricing for all projects regardless of a country's economic rating.

Caribbean Development Bank (CDB)

The CDB also receives some funding from the IDB to fund their projects, focused on promoting socioeconomic development throughout the region. According to the CDB website, it awards about US$50 million toward these projects, which includes the procurement of consulting services. The CDB websites includes a procurement portal where individuals and businesses can register so that they will have access specifically to CDB projects.

---

* Bahamas, Barbados, Belize, Bolivia, Costa Rica, the Dominican Republic, Ecuador, El Salvador, Guatemala, Guyana, Haiti, Honduras, Jamaica, Nicaragua, Panama, Paraguay, Suriname, Trinidad and Tobago, and Uruguay. The remaining borrowing member countries include Argentina, Brazil, Chile, Colombia, Mexico, Peru, and Venezuela.

African Development Bank (AfDB)

The AfDB, which began operating in 1964 and whose headquarters are in Abidjan, Côte d'Ivoire, presents another opportunity for companies looking to provide services throughout the continent of Africa. Within the AfDB exists the General Services and Procurement Department, which handles purchasing services and goods that support their mandate as outlined in their sustainable development goals, some of which includes eliminating poverty, gender equality, and environmental preservation. The AfDB consists of 80 member countries—54 regional members and 26 non-regional members—the latter of which includes Asian, European, Latin American, Middle Eastern, and North American countries. The non-regional members, which were allowed beginning in 1982, provide additional financial resources to the AfDB's efforts. The projects range from a variety of areas, such as health, education, and telecommunications, thus, presenting opportunities for service providers. Other opportunities with the AfDB include activities that emphasize policy-based reforms, technical assistance, and policy advice.

Asian Development Bank (ADB)

The ADB, which was created in 1966, also focuses on getting rid of the dire poverty that plagues many countries throughout the Asian and Pacific regions through technical assistance programs and grants, among others. Any service providers interested in projects pertaining to socioeconomic development can find opportunities with this particular MDB. The ADB has 68 members, 49 of which are regional members. India received the most in terms of financial and technical assistance commitments with close to US$48 billion. The greatest number of projects as a part of this commitment have been designated for China with 1,229 projects, according to public corporate data. The high level of commitment to India and China presents numerous opportunities, including for service-providers. Other countries that have a large number of projects include Indonesia, Pakistan, Bangladesh, the Philippines, and Vietnam.

A number of active projects, particularly for consulting services, continued throughout 2020. Shorter projects of approximately one month or more have budgets of tens of thousands of dollars.

UK Department for International Development (DFID)

DFID is a UK government agency that funds development projects around the world. In June 2020, the UK Prime Minister publicly announced that

DFID would merge with the Foreign Office, which focuses on diplomatic affairs, in an effort to become more effective within the international development community. The merger was completed in September 2020. The DFID website includes its own portal that makes it easy to find contracts and register to partner with the government as a supplier.

European Investment Bank (EIB)

The EIB is unique compared to the other MDBs in that it is an investment bank and a global development bank. The EIB consists of the 27 member EU states. Many of the EIB's funded projects span throughout the European Union focused on economic development and integration within the EU. Furthermore, the EIB funds projects in regions and countries beyond the EU and Europe. For instance, the EIP funds projects throughout the Caribbean region focused on private sector development, infrastructure, and climate action.

This chapter has highlighted two mechanisms for identifying market opportunities. The first set of opportunities can be found in those markets with which a service supplier's home country has signed a reciprocal trade agreement. Trade deals allow for ease of access, lower the cost of doing business in that market, and offer a dispute settlement process should members violate the terms of the trade agreement. The second set of opportunities rest with grants and contracts funded by federal governments and multilateral development banks.

CASE STUDY 5.1 HELPING COMPANIES ESTABLISH A PHYSICAL PRESENCE IN MEXICO

"There's a lot of opportunity.... All you have to do is come down and participate, and you're going to learn and see that we've got all of these U.S. companies who are operating along the border who need the same services that they need on the U.S. side."

Veronica Contreras, President, Zaveros Consulting

Veronica Contreras, president of Zavero Consulting, Inc., offers consultation services to manufacturers who are interested in establishing an operation in Mexico. She says, "My specific role is to help companies to understand the cost of setting up an operation in Mexico, understanding the process, understanding the timeline, and helping them put together the right path for their journey." Ms. Contreras, who is based in Southern California, has been in the industry for two decades and has set up 50 companies in Mexico. Many of her clients are in the manufacturing sector and within the services sector, specifically from the call-center industry.

Although Ms. Contreras runs a small consulting firm, she is a part of a shelter services company, Co-Production International (CPI). She works with CPI to assist global manufacturing companies set up in Mexico under the Maquiladora Shelter Program. The shelter services program in Mexico allows the shelter company to handle the administrative and legal requirements for setting up a business while the foreign company can focus on manufacturing. In other words, the shelter company eliminates the red tape and bureaucratic procedures for the foreign manufacturing company while also serving as the legal entity for compliance matters.

Ms. Contreras' strategy for reaching clients in the United States and other markets outside of Mexico includes several types of activities—referrals, marketing, speaking, training, and collaborations. The first strategy has been to maintain connection with former clients who have moved to other companies and/or have become presidents and owners of manufacturing facilities. The referrals from many of these connections have predominantly been instrumental in helping Ms. Contreras with continuing to attract new clients and taking on additional projects.

Additionally, marketing has been key to reaching the target companies in the manufacturing sector and the call-center industry.

> We do a lot of marketing, just general marketing. So, we have a very detailed profile of what we are looking for and who is the right candidate for evaluating Mexico. We basically have a database that helps understand who those companies are ... and we are constantly feeding them information like white papers and whatever information that might be interesting to them to serve them where, eventually, if the time isn't right now, at some point they are going to look at Mexico as a possibility. So we want to be in front of them ... when that happens.

Another set of activities that has helped Ms. Contreras reach clients looking to expand to the Mexican market has been sharing knowledge and expertise through public speaking and webinars. Also, collaborations with attorneys and consultants who are also looking at similar markets has helped her to reach additional potential clients interested in expanding to the Mexican market.

What are some of the traits of the clients that have used Zavero Consulting to set up in Mexico? Ms. Contreras explained that many of the companies that she works with are between US$20 million and US$2 billion companies. A company under US$10 million has faced a series of challenges in sustaining their operations in both the United States and Mexico. The typical client is a larger manufacturing company that is not shutting down an operation in the United States but one that is expanding its operations to Mexico. In this scenario, the emphasis is on a consulting service in the United States that helps U.S. manufacturers expand to another market—Mexico.

What opportunities have been made available specifically for those clients in today's global economy? The U.S.–China trade war has made Mexico an attractive market because of the increased costs of doing business in China and the market access offered through the USMCA.* Ms. Contreras shares:

> I would say right now that we have some Chinese companies who are evaluating setting up in Mexico because of the [U.S.]-China trade war. They were impacted, and they see the writing on the wall, at least, for the next couple of years. They are the ones who are evaluating setting up their own investments in Mexico to serve the U.S. market by having Mexican operations.

The manufacturing clients also benefit from the changes brought about by the USMCA, especially regarding the introduction of digital technologies to the trade process and reform measures put in place in Mexico. Ms. Contreras goes further to say:

> For the manufacturing industry, [the USMCA] has been a deal changer from everything to having a smart border and having congruency even with the United States' borders. So, we have a ton of different accesses into the U.S. The process could be different in New York than it was in Long Beach. All of this is now standardized, as well as Mexico following suit. [Mexico was] already working toward this prior to the USMCA, but it forced the Mexican government to start becoming more digital in all areas, and that

---

* For specific data on this trend, see Cantera (2020) and "New trade deal expected to fuel invasion of Asian parts manufacturers" 2020 https://mexiconewsdaily.com/news/trade-deal-expected-to-fuel-invasion-of-parts-manufacturers/.

wasn't the case before. Before, you had to physically go to the office. There was no digital signature. Now … everything is digital.

Additionally, Mexico has implemented labor and tax reforms that impact the manufacturing sector in the country.*

The USMCA talks and implementation also had an impact on Ms. Contreras' consulting services. She mentioned:

> The fact that there was a threat out there for the last few years that they could cancel NAFTA altogether created a lot of uncertainty … so a lot of my projects that were going to set up in Mexico were frozen because of that uncertainty. The fact that the USMCA has now been signed has eliminated uncertainty and has opened the gates for companies to move forward with their projects.

There are key recommendations that Ms. Contreras shares to help companies, specifically services-based companies, looking to offer services internationally.

> They need to join the chamber of commerce and participate both in the U.S. and Mexico side … in order for them to learn and understand how to take advantage of international services and figure out how to plug themselves in…. [U.S. companies in Mexico] want to see it in their language because they want to implement these concepts that don't exist in Mexico. It's not that they don't exist, it's that they need more sophistication, for example, human resources, consultants in H.R., and everything from just elevating the workforce and ensuring less turnovers … all of those issues that are in the U.S., Mexico has them too. And there's [fewer] service providers to serve the market in a way that an American company would like to see it!

Even with these opportunities, the main challenge that service providers, particularly U.S. service providers, face is that local problems in Mexico are solved by U.S. decision-makers with a U.S.-based solution that may not necessarily translate into success in Mexico, according to Ms. Contreras.

---

* See Brin (2020) for more on the USMCA and labor reform measures in Mexico.

In closing, Ms. Contreras adds, "Mexico is an amazing country to do business in for both manufacturing and call center industries and is very well structured from a business perspective in regards to control and processes …. It is not scary but different."

Bibliography

Acharya, Nish. 2015. "Where the TPP misses the mark for small business and entrepreneurs." November 6.

AmCham Shanghai. *Market Barriers for American Firms in China*. 2018. Shanghai, China: The American Chamber of Commerce in Shanghai.

Brin, Dinah Wisenberg. 2020. US-Mexico-Canada Agreement Introduces Labor Changes. Accessed October 1, 2020. https://www.shrm.org/resourcesandtools/hr-topics/global-hr/pages/usmca-introduces-labor-changes.aspx.

Cantera, Sara. 2020. "T-MEC abre una puerta a firmas chinas en México." El Universal, 1–8. Accessed September 23, 2020. https://www.eluniversal.com.mx/cartera/china-mete-acelerador-en-invasion-de-autopartes-mexico.

Christensen, Sandra L. 1993. "Is there a role for small business in the North American free trade area?" Business Forum, 44–46.

DFID (Department for International Development). n.d. "Prime Minister announces merger of Department for International Development and Foreign Office." Accessed September 9, 2020. https://www.gov.uk/search/news-and-communications?

International Trade Administration. n.d. "Brazil – Country commercial guide." Accessed October 1, 2020. https://www.trade.gov/knowledge-product/brazil-selling-government-brazil.

International Trade Centre. n.d. *Trade Map*. https://www.trademap.org/.

Jackimovicz, Alex. 2015. TPP would damage Maine small businesses and communities. Beacon. Accessed September 6, 2020. https://mainebeacon.com/tpp-would-damage-maine-small-businesses-and-communities/.

Lewis, Charles; and Margaret Ebrahim. 1993. "Can Mexico and big business USA buy NAFTA?" *The Nation*, June 14, 826–839.

Marks, Gene. 2016. "Why small businesses don't like the Trans-Pacific Partnership agreement." *The Washington Post*, November 9.

Morita-Jaeger, Minako; and Ingo Borchert. 2020. *The Representation of SME Interests in Free Trade Agreements: Recommendations for Best Practice*. UK Trade Policy Observatory, University of Sussex, Federation of Small Businesses. Brighton, United Kingdom.

"New trade deal expected to fuel invasion of Asian parts manufacturers." 2020. *Mexico News Daily*, 1–3.

Rosenbaum, Eric. 2019. 1 in 5 companies say China has stolen their IP within the last year: CNBC CFO survey. *CNBC*.

"The EIB in the Caribbean: priorities and projects." 2016. Luxembourg and Santo Domingo, Dominican Republic: European Investment Bank. https://www.eib.org/attachments/country/eib_in_caribbean_en.pdf.

"The Theft of American Intellectual Property: Reassessments of the Challenge and United States Policy." 2017. In *IP Commission Report*, edited by The Commission on the Theft of American Intellectual Property. Seattle, WA: The National Bureau of Asian Research.

Thomson Reuters International and KPMG. 2015. *Seventy Percent of Companies Do Not Fully Utilize Free Trade Agreements, According to Thomson Reuters-KPMG International Survey*. Thomas Reuters. Accessed October 5, 2020. https://www.thomsonreuters.com/en/press-releases/2015/november/seventy-percent-of-companies-do-not-fully-utilize-free-trade-agreements.html

Trans-Pacific Partnership (TPP) Agreement, Office of the U.S. n.d. *Trade Representative*. https://ustr.gov/trade-agreements/free-trade-agreements/trans-pacific-partnership/tpp-full-text.

USITC (U.S. International Trade Commission). 2010. *Small and Medium-sized Enterprises: Characteristics and Performance*. Washington, DC: USITC Publication.

USMCA (United States- Mexico-Canada Agreement). n.d. Office of the U.S. Trade Representative. https://ustr.gov/trade-agreements/free-trade-agreements/united-states-mexico-canada-agreement/agreement-between.

USMCA. n.d. *United States-Mexico-Canada Trade Fact Sheet: Modernizing NAFTA into a 21st Century Trade Agreement*. Washington, DC: Office of the U.S. Trade Representative.

USTR (U.S. Trade Representatives) Office. n.d. "Brazil." USTR. https://ustr.gov/countries-regions/americas/brazil.

World Bank. n.d. "Brazil: Overview." Accessed October 1, 2020. https://www.worldbank.org/en/country/brazil/overview.

Zumbrun, Josh. 2019. "What Can the U.S. Sell China? Services." Wall Street Journal. https://www.wsj.com/articles/what-can-the-u-s-sell-china-services-11548887498.

Chapter 6

Selecting an Export Market

Following a workshop for small business owners on conducting international market research the right way in Southern California, one of the attendees shared how he did not secure a deal for a well-established company that sought international market research. The attendee did not get business, because he did not know how to provide in-depth, useful research for that potential client. The attendee submitted a report based on a general internet search. As that attendee discovered, the challenge with relying on a basic internet search is that one must wade through a sea of data, have an awareness of exactly which piece of information is relevant, and know how to properly interpret that information.

Of course, a company will not pay for information that is readily available online. Instead, the added value for any company looking to identify an export market is to gain access to information collected in a systematic way through the use of tools, resources, and methodologies that go beyond the confines of the World Wide Web. (Yes. Even the World Wide Web does not capture all possible information. Furthermore, all information published on the internet is not accurate.) Although the example of the workshop attendee pertained to research to help a company export a product, the same principle applies to using detailed research and statistical analysis to select the best market for a service.

This chapter presents a step-by-step guide for identifying and selecting the best export market for a service. This chapter also shows exactly what these steps look like, how they should be used in the selection process, how to use the available resources, and why the steps are important for a firm's ability to export competitively. Following the approach laid out in this chapter has saved companies time and energy in the long term, as well as frustration, while leaving them with a laser-focused strategy to guide the implementation phase afterward.

Step #1: Assess the Company's Resources and Capabilities

Entering the global market is a marathon rather than a sprint. Any marathon runner must spend months preparing adequately, training properly, and checking his/her health status before embarking on a 26.2 mile (42.195 km) run in order to reach the finish line in great shape. In other words, preparation reduces the chance for serious injuries and a longer, more painful recovery period. The same goes for the planning stages of exporting a service. A firm must first conduct a detailed, honest assessment of its health by completing the standard Strengths-Weaknesses-Opportunities-Threats (SWOT) analysis. While many individuals in the area of business may be familiar with the SWOT analysis, there still needs to be clarity as to what information should be included for each analytical point so that it is relevant and useful to the specific firm and its service. When carrying out a SWOT analysis, here are some questions to ask about one's firm and what to look for when answering these questions:

What are the Company's Strengths?

High name and brand recognition. The business owner and/or executives must measure the degree to which the firm's name and brand garner recognition from its target market in the home country. The same questions that would be posed to anyone trying to sell a good in the overseas market applies to the services sector, as well. Being able to demonstrate the ability to become an easily recognizable brand within the target market shows that the company can demonstrate that it can be successful in its home country. Although success in the home country does not automatically translate into success in any given foreign country, it can be a starting point when looking at how to devise a strategy within the international context.

Strong client base. Having a solid client base refers to growing the number of clients, especially repeat clients, for whom the company has provided a service. Those clients could be individuals, other companies, the government, and/or educational institutions. Assessing the client base entails reviewing the company's track record with these clients and looking at areas that can be improved upon and/or applied to the target client base in an overseas market.

Adequate cash flow and financial resources. Having sound financials, in which a company has consistent revenue from the domestic market, helps when making the transition to selling a service overseas. In other words, it is important for a company looking to export overseas to have a budget for properly carrying out the different components of the export process from planning to implementation. Some items to consider and gauge the cost for quality work include research, travel, staff, marketing material, local experts, and complying with the local laws, etc. in the export market under consideration.

Adequate human capital. A company that has developed a team with the appropriate and applicable talent, skills, knowledge, and expertise for an international expansion will have greater success in exporting to international markets. The more specific skills, etc. required include having substantive knowledge of a specific region or country(ies) and proficient or fluent language skills associated with the potential export market, if different from that of the home country. Hiring a full-time in-house team of individuals with the proper expertise, seeking a third-party organization that brings the proper tools to export a service successfully, or a mixture of both remain among the ingredients necessary to sustain the company internationally.

Focused differentiation strategy. A company must be able to communicate effectively as to how its service differs from that of its competitors and meet the needs of its consumers or clients. Whereas the differentiation strategy in the home market may have led to firm growth, that firm will have to consider the need to adapt or completely change its strategy to succeed in another country.

Adaptability. Changes in the home market may require a company to be able to adjust and adapt rapidly in order to remain competitive in an ever-changing economic environment while staying true to its core mission and values. A firm that has a strategy that allows for flexibility would have the same capabilities when developing a strategy that would be appropriate to a completely different environment.

Use of technology. A company that takes advantage of the technology, such as digital technology, to gain a wider reach far more effectively will benefit from being able to attract customers and clients from beyond its national borders. Technology in and of itself is not a strategy. Rather, it is a tool for fulfilling a strategy. Nevertheless, the easier access, even with the use of technology, still requires the proper research and strategy.

What are the Company's Weaknesses?

Little to no name and brand recognition. A firm that has not built an effective strategy that would lead to much name or brand recognition in its home market may find it difficult to just jump to an overseas market and sell its services successfully. Expanding to the overseas market should be an effort to widen its brand's reach rather than to compensate for the inability to succeed in the home market.

Weak client base. A company that has not succeeded in building a loyal base of clients or, at least, having a list of clients or customers with whom it has successfully provided a service may find it challenging to do so in a foreign market. The key idea to keep in mind is that shifting the business strategy to a global business strategy is not a panacea for the inability to develop a solid client base at any point in time in the home market.

Deficient cash flow and financial resources. Engaging in the export process entails several steps from research and planning to developing a strategy and implementation. Without a consistent revenue stream that can be budgeted for the export process, a company will not be able to export in a successful and sustainable manner. It is equally important that business owners remain truly honest about the financial health of the company when considering expanding its sales to the global market.

Limited human capital. Companies with minimal resources may try to expand globally with individuals who may assist with growing the company domestically but do not have the appropriate skills to take the company globally. In the case of many smaller firms, the business owner that has not been trained in market research or is unaware of the right tools for doing so may fall short of conducting substantive, useful, and appropriate research. Misplaced skills and expertise can prove extremely costly over the long term.

Lack of a differentiation strategy. The inability to articulate how a services-based company is distinct from its competitors in the home market will only translate into a premature, costly attempt to expand to a foreign market.

Inability to adapt. A company that lacks the tools, resources, and talent to adjust and adapt quickly to the changes in the forces of nature—which can be political, economic, legal, or social—in the home country will not find it any easier to do so in the international market.

Technologically inept. A company that sticks to the traditional methods of attracting and retaining its client base will remain restricted to the confines of those methods. Those methods may include word of mouth, cold-calling, face-to-face meetings, and use of paper copy and regular mail as a part of the business processes to generate leads. At the same time, the business does not invest in the technology that would reduce the costs, both in terms of time and money, associated with these processes. In the long run, the traditional method may cost a firm business and growth opportunities.

For instance, even in the 21st century, some business owners may discredit the value of a professionally designed, user-friendly website in promoting their services to their clients in the home market. According to a 2017 CNBC/Survey Monkey Small Business Survey, 45% of respondents admitted that they do not have a website for their business, because they depend on word of mouth alone. Of the small businesses that do have a website, only 36% communicate news to their customers or potential customers (Rosenbaum 2019). Consequently, this type of business is missing out on attracting potential clients beyond the reach of their word-of-mouth referral network.

Other business owners may resist the digital technology that provides simple, easy tools that allow for virtual face-to-face meetings with existing and potential clients from all over the world; phone calls to clients without a charge; electronic document sharing and signing; secure payment systems; and communication through newsletters and video posts. Finally, the failure to invest time to learn about the online software that reduce the normal effort required to complete transactions, such as timing communication with others (e.g., Hootsuite), scheduling meetings (e.g., Calendly), and organizing outreach efforts (e.g., HubSpot, Salesforce), costs the business owner an enormous amount of time in the long run. Although technology may assist a business in having a further reach in the international market, it is still important to tailor the use of technology to the sophistication of and levels of access in the technological environment of the market under consideration.

What Relevant Opportunities Exist in the International Market?

Fact-based, in-depth customized market research helps a company to identify the opportunities, two of which were also discussed at length in the previous chapter, that are available in an export market that may make access easier.

Trade policies. Trade policies at the international, regional, and national levels present opportunities for businesses to expand much more easily to another market. Those trade policies may come in the form of reciprocal trade agreements, which are trade deals negotiated between two or more countries with the goal of ensuring reciprocal access to each other's markets. Such market access comes in the form of the reduction of tariffs, removal of quotas, and the elimination of regulatory barriers to trade between the member countries. Some of the key issues in a reciprocal trade agreement that pertain to service providers include market access via the elimination of quotas, intellectual property, e-commerce, and dispute settlement.

Digital trade plays an important role in the provision and delivery of services globally. Digital trade is addressed to varying degrees in multilateral trade deals (Wu 2017). Many of these deals address digital trade by including an e-commerce chapter. E-commerce refers to goods and digital products sold online, internet services, and medical or professional services that are delivered via the internet (Chander 2018). However, in 2020, the 26-year old NAFTA was replaced by the USMCA, which created an even stronger, comprehensive framework in the area of digital trade (Chander 2018; Matthews 2019; Beckerman 2020). "The new Digital Trade chapter contains the strongest disciplines on digital trade of any international agreement, providing a firm foundation for the expansion of trade and investment in the innovative products and services where the United States has a competitive advantage," writes the Office of U.S. Trade Representatives (USTR). With digital trade playing a significant role in allowing service providers from healthcare to education to offer services to a wider portion of the global population and at a faster rate, the framework set by the USMCA for other trade deals, as well as existing provisions for services in general, present opportunities in the United States, Canadian, and Mexican markets.

As an exporter, narrowing down a market, where access would be much easier and the risks lower, should begin with those countries that have signed trade deals with the home country.

Funded projects. International financial institutions (IFIs) and multilateral development banks (MDBs) offer funding through contracts and grants that will allow any-sized firm to provide a service in a foreign country, as also discussed in the previous chapter. The transparent process mitigates the risks, which would be far greater when trying to enter another market alone. Many of the service-oriented projects that receive this type of funding are in the emerging market, developing, and least-developed economies. Each project will have a specific focus, for example, building the capacity for women farmers to export their products or improving waste management practices to protect the health of the local population. Project funding can be a source for selecting a market to export a service in an efficient and less risky manner. Many of these opportunities can be found at grants.gov and the System for Award Management (SAM) (sam.gov).

Existence of a need and demand. As with operating a business domestically, resources are available that help one to measure the current level of demand or need in another country. The trends in trade and investment show where there is a demand in the potential export market, which presents an opportunity for a service provider to satisfy that demand.

At the same time, there may be a need that has not yet been addressed effectively or at all, which may also highlight an opportunity to enter another market. In-depth research about the market helps one to fully understand the story behind the trends to determine whether a service exported to a foreign country will have an increased chance for sustainable success.

One tool that can serve as a starting point for looking at the trends of which services are being purchased and sold to different countries around the world is the Trade Map database. This database is presented by the International Trade Centre and consists of data collected from the United Nations and the World Trade Organization. For instance, a U.S.-based financial services company may consider Japan as a potential export market because of the 2020 trade agreement between the United States and Japan and the fact that the trade deal includes provisions pertaining to digital trade. The U.S.-Japan digital trade provisions make data localization requirements illegal, including for foreign service suppliers. The same U.S.-based financial service company can use the Trade Map database to see the most recent trends in U.S.–Japan financial services trade (Table 6.1).

According to the available data, U.S. exports of financial services to Japan showed steady growth from US$2.4 billion to US$2.9 billion over a three-year period.[*]

Non-U.S. companies can also use the database to complete the same exercise and study the trends in specific services-based industries and a foreign country of interest.

Collaborators. When studying new markets, it is important to look at competitors. It is also useful to identify collaborators in that market. Collaborating with firms and individuals in the local market may help to reduce the costs associated with making mistakes due to limited

---

[*] For the most recent data, these figures are based on those recorded for Japan's import of financial services from the United States among other countries.

Table 6.1   U.S. Export of Financial Services to Japan (2015–2018) (US$thousand)

Source: International Trade Centre Trade Map

understanding of that market. Collaboration may allow new firms to pool resources and boost their ability to compete over the long term in an export market.

What are the Threats Against My Firm in the International Market?

In addition to identifying the opportunities, a serious assessment gets beyond the fantasy that one can enter the market in less than six months and see quick financial returns or that the strategy that works in the home country will automatically transfer successfully to a foreign market. Rather, an honest assessment of one's firm within the international context will look at the potential threats and risks in the countries under consideration to determine which international market(s) would be less feasible to access.

Strong competition. A market with a few strong local competitors or saturated with both local and international competitors will present a challenge to one's market entry and competitiveness strategy. Therefore, it is important to adequately assess the landscape in that country.

Protectionist microeconomic policies. A market may be attractive because of its large population and/or economic size. However, high tariff and regulatory barriers may make that market more difficult to access thus, increasing a firm's cost of doing business in that market. Service providers do not have to worry about tariffs being imposed during cross-border trade. However, other non-tariff barriers, such as regulatory barriers, may make it more difficult to access a foreign market. For instance, a country may require that a foreign firm enter a joint venture and hold minority share to operate in that market. Such a requirement adds to a firm's costs in areas such as the loss of intellectual property. Additionally, government policies that attempt to limit competition from foreign service providers in favor of local producers also present a challenge for a firm looking to expand to the overseas market. Discriminatory policies and practices reduce choice for consumers, result in higher prices, and lead to inefficiencies in the local market.

In a 2019 report, the USTR mentioned that some of its trading partners—China, Japan, and the European Union (EU)—continue to impose trade barriers to foreign service providers. Some of those barriers consist of China's January 2019 e-commerce law, which make it difficult for China's e-commerce platforms to be held liable for selling counterfeit products; Japan's regulation of the express delivery, insurance, financial, legal, telecommunications, and renewable energy services; and the European Union's tax on digital service providers with worldwide revenues surpassing US$849 million. The USTR report was published the same year that the United States eventually finalized a trade deal with Japan; engaged China in trade talks, which led to the signing of the first phase of the U.S.–China trade deal in January 2020; and began preparations for trade talks with the United Kingdom, which began in May 2020 following the United Kingdom's official exit from the EU five months earlier. The existence of a trade deal between two or more countries removes many of the discriminatory regulatory barriers and unfair trade practices. Without a trade agreement, a firm may find the process similar to running a marathon in the hot sun without any water, thus making the journey extremely arduous.

Shifts in political and/or economic conditions. Negative changes in political and economic conditions have a serious impact on a company's ability to thrive over the long term. For this reason, it is important to not just assess the current situation in a single market, but to collect data on forecasts based on solid, in-depth research to determine the right export market, entry strategy, and alternative markets.

For example, political and economic changes in China have impacted companies across all sectors—agriculture, manufacturing, and services. The growing influence of the labor movement in China led to an increase in the costs of labor, thus reducing the country's cost competitiveness. The U.S.–China trade tensions have also led to practices restricting the import and export of goods and services between the countries. Regarding the services trade between the United States and China, U.S. services exports to China have declined drastically. According to the US-China Business Council's (USCBC) *2020 State Export Report*, although U.S. services exports have seen tremendous growth from US$16.8 billion in 2009 to US$55.3 billion in 2018, year to year growth has slowed down. From 2016 to 2018, U.S. services exports overall increased by only 2%. Not only did expansion to the United States' other large markets—United Kingdom and Canada—contribute to the lower figures, the trade tensions have also played a role, according to the same USCBC's report. By 2017–18, only 15 states were able to export more than US$1 billion in services to China.

Many analysts anticipated a significant decline in the enrollment of additional international students at U.S. universities during the 2020–21 academic year. Those same analysts argued that U.S. immigration policies and the visa application process have made it harder for students to pursue their university studies in the United States, thus leading to a drop in enrollment. The estimated enrollment reduction was anywhere from 63% to 98% during the 2020–21 academic year when compared to that of 2018–19 (Rampell 2020).

Sudden changes in client behavior. Another factor to consider when selecting an export market is any shifts in the behavior of consumers in that market, which may either harm or help sales. The severe blow to the global economy in 2020 due to the health pandemic demonstrates the quickness with which consumer behavior can shift. For example, McKinsey and Company reported five recurring observations of consumer behavior throughout 45 countries: (1) shift to value and essentials, (2) flight to digital and omnichannel, (3) shock to loyalty, (4) emphasis on health and "caring" economy, and (5) growth of the homebody economy (Arora et al. 2020).

The results were based on surveys in the United States, Brazil, South Africa, the United Kingdom, France, Germany, Spain, Italy, India, Japan, South Korea, and China. Participants from all of the countries, except for India, said that they would spend less on pet-care services. In terms of fitness and wellness, survey respondents in India and China mentioned that they would spend more, whereas those in the remaining countries indicated that they would spend less. When it comes to personal-care service, respondents in all 12 countries mentioned that they would spend less on personal-care services. In other services-related industries, such as food take-out/delivery, short-term home rentals, domestic and international flights, and hotel stays, an overwhelming majority of respondents mentioned that they would cut spending (Arora et al. 2020).

Future technological changes. The year 2020 alone demonstrated the impact of technological changes on companies. Those services-based firms that resisted the technological advances that allowed for virtual meetings, showcasing services and expertise, streamlining processes, and facilitating smoother transactions found themselves playing catch up, facing a steeper learning curve, and having to also transition along with clients than those companies that were already prepared. The global health pandemic forced the use of technology. Those firms already technologically savvy could continue with low overhead and at a higher rate of speed in terms of reaching potential clients overseas.

Although this list for the different components of the SWOT analysis is certainly not exhaustive, it provides a basic framework for conducting the proper analysis within the context of exporting a service to any given market overseas.

Step #2: Research the Market

As the marathon runner that must be aware of the external factors that may affect performance, such as the weather conditions and the terrain, the company looking to export a service to the international market should also gather information on the external environment. Having a fact-based understanding of the international market helps one to develop an appropriate strategy. As simple as this may sound, many companies attempt to enter foreign markets without first conducting research. A sound strategy is built through investing the time and money in detailed, fact-based, credible research on a market to: 1) determine the best market for the firm's service, or 2) identify key services to consider exporting to a specific market of interest. Unlike research pertaining to the cross-border trade in manufactured goods and agricultural commodities, services-based trade data is sparse. As a result, services firms will have to conduct additional research using various strategies, resources, and tools. One database that serves as a starting point and that has been mentioned previously is Trade Map, which consists of statistics collected from the United Nations and the World Trade Organization, as a part of the International Trade Centre. Trade Map offers basic insight into the trends in cross-border trade in services from which to build, although the data is not in real-time.

Gathering information on the top markets for consideration for a service firm's exports requires deeper insight into what contributes to more or less stability at any given time. Using the statistical databases on understanding trends, the potential export market can be identified by looking at the top export markets for a specific service in terms of dollar value or other currency over a period of time. Secondly, the annual percentage of growth shows which potential export markets are growing quickly. The research shared here goes beyond the numbers to emphasize gathering information that tells the story behind the numbers. In other words, to fully understand the journey ahead, a PESTLE (Political, Economic, Sociocultural, Technological, Legal, and Environmental) analysis serves as a roadmap.

Political. The political conditions of a country may present an opportunity or a threat to a business looking to export its service internationally. For this reason, it is important to do extensive research that includes some level of understanding of the relevant political history of a country, current political environment, and future forecasts that could impact the company's ability to compete in that market. As an example, an individual exporter in the food manufacturing and service industries needed research and a strategic plan that would assist in his efforts to export an agricultural product from the West African country of Cote d'Ivoire to the United States to manufacture into a snack for U.S. consumers. As a part of an international trade research training program for undergraduate business students, a supplemental research report was completed, which focused on exporting from the United States to Cote d'Ivoire. The first instinct of the researchers-in-training was to grab all data from the internet that goes as far back as the establishment of the political system in the country. While much of the data about the country's political history and current political system were interesting and informative, placing the data into context and explaining what it means for the individual exporter becomes more useful toward building a sustainable competitive strategy. For instance, following a 1999 coup d'état, civil war broke out and plagued the country until a peace agreement was signed in 2007. Political instability and violence followed again after the disputed presidential election in 2011. As a result, many businesses lost confidence in a country that once boasted significant economic growth from its cocoa exports. Years later, the country was still in the process of restoring business confidence, trying to attract investment, and growing economically following such a long period of conflict.

By the time the research training program took place, business confidence and investment in the country were restored. Additionally, the African Development Bank began offering funding to the country once again. The final analysis based on the contemporary political situation was that the exporter could offer the food services without fear of disruption due to political instability, at least for the moment.

The individual exporter who was already in the process of setting up a food service business found the one-year forecast based on the information available at the time to be useful. By the end of 2019, news reports and analyses highlighted the potential impact that the October 2020 presidential elections would have on Cote d'Ivoire's political stability, which, in turn, would affect business confidence and foreign direct investment. A final analysis highlighted what this meant for the exporter, and the information was built into a strategy so that the exporter could be as prepared as possible for any changes in the country's political situation.

The World Bank's Worldwide Governance Indicators (WGI) serve as a credible source for assessing the political environment in countries around the globe. The WGI measures political risk in the areas of accountability, political stability, government effectiveness, regulatory quality, rule of law, and control of corruption. Each country is given a final rank compared to countries around the world and an individual score, in which the higher numbers represent better governance. For example, in the case of Cote d'Ivoire in 2018, its governance- related scores range from −0.22 to −0.93 (Figure 6.1).

The country's percentile rank, per indicators related to governance, ranges from 15.71% to 46.15%, with a margin of error of less than 1% (Figure 6.2).

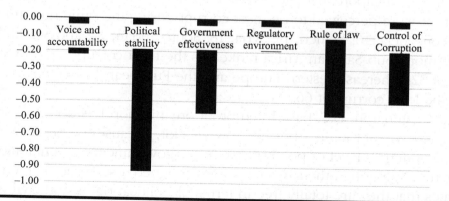

Figure 6.1   Cote d'Ivoire Governance-related Scores (2018). Source: World Development Indicators

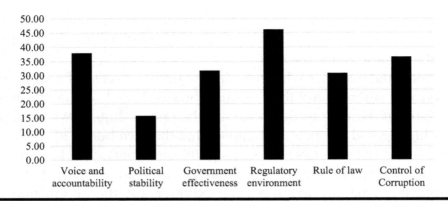

Figure 6.2   Cote d'Ivoire Governance Percentile Rank (2018). Source: World Development Indicators

Nevertheless, it is still important to conduct research that tells the story behind the final scores and rankings, such as that mentioned earlier about the political instability caused by Cote d'Ivoire's civil war.

Transparency International, a Berlin-based non-governmental organization, offers the complimentary, online corruption perceptions index. The index is based on responses by experts and business executives from all around the world regarding how they perceive the levels of public sector corruption in 180 countries and territories. The corruption level in each country and territory is scored from 0 (highly corrupt) to 100 (minimal, if any, levels of corruption).

In 2019, Transparency International reported that the average country score was 43. The five countries with the highest score, or that were perceived to be the least corrupt, were Denmark, 87; New Zealand, 87; Finland, 86; Singapore, 85; and Sweden, 85. The countries that ranked the lowest, or were perceived to be most corrupt during the same time frame, were Venezuela, 16; Yemen, 15; Syria, 13; South Sudan, 12; and Somalia, 9. Furthermore, Sub-Saharan Africa ranked as the most corrupt region with a score of 32, whereas Western Europe and the European Union were found to be the least corrupt at 66.

The Washington, D.C.-based non-profit organization Freedom House also serves as a useful tool in a business owner's kit, because the organization tracks a country's level of political openness, government accountability, and transparency, among others. Countries are assigned a score up to 100 that indicates that they are totally free in terms of political rights and civil liberties. The lower the number, the less free that country is.

"Corruption threatens the integrity of markets, undermines fair competition, distorts resources allocation, destroys public trust, and undermines the rule of law," according to the International Chamber of Commerce (ICC). The ICC represents the private sector at the global level and focuses on combating corruption to create a free and fair business environment. Corruption pervades developed and developing economies. Companies pay a bribe in return for orders and government contracts, thus beating out other companies that may be more competitive (Heimann 1997, 147). The World Economic Forum estimates the cost of corruption in 2011 at over 5% of global GDP (US$2.6 trillion) with over US$1 trillion paid in bribes each year.

Finally, the internal policies of a country regarding any restrictions on imports and exports and political relations between trade partners can have an impact on business owners. The role of politics and policies became even more evident in recent years with U.S. tariff increases on steel and aluminum, retaliatory policies on U.S. agricultural goods by countries such as China and Mexico, and restrictions on the export of personal protective equipment and certain pharmaceuticals in response to the COVID-19 pandemic. These examples focus on goods. However, such an approach also spilled over into the services area.

For example, U.S. services companies, in the areas of lodging, financial services, and entertainment, began tapping into the Cuban market when former U.S. President Barack Obama loosened restrictions to allow for increased trade with Cuba, following his December 2014 announcement. However, much of the progress toward normalizing diplomatic and economic relations with Cuba was rolled back with a shift in policy by U.S. President Donald Trump after he officially took office on January 20, 2017.

Tensions surrounding China's policies toward foreign businesses have created a challenge for service suppliers. China's legislation in the areas of intellectual property and requirements of forming a joint venture with a local company are areas in which a foreign company must be aware when considering this market for exporting its services.

Economic. The macroeconomic conditions and microeconomic relations affect the ability for individual firms to succeed in an overseas market, thus playing a role in the selection of an export market.

For U.S. companies, two of the closest countries geographically—Canada and Mexico—present opportunities beyond geographical proximity. A long-established trade policy deepening economic integration under the North

American Free Trade Agreement (NAFTA), which was replaced by the United States-Mexico-Canada Agreement (USMCA) on July 1, 2020, creates opportunities for service providers throughout the North American market.

For instance, Mexico currently offers market access to 46 countries from regions all around the world, except for the African region, through the removal of tariff and regulatory barriers on particular goods and services. However, its first major trade deal was NAFTA, which included provisions to liberalize the services-based telecommunications industry. The Mexican telecommunications industry was a nine-billion-dollar industry within a year of NAFTA taking effect (Aleman 2001). Even with NAFTA, the agreement did little to further the privatization of the industry in Mexico, as evident by the challenges that AT&T and MCI WorldCom faced when trying to provide services to the Mexican market (Aleman 2001). (MCI WorldCom has since been bought out by Verizon in 2006.) Rather, the industry continued to be monopolized by Teléfones de Mexico, S.A., often referred to as Telmex. Telmex has been led by Carlos Slim, who was listed as the wealthiest person in the world most recently in 2014. Furthermore, questions surrounding cross-border services and foreign investment in basic communications were not addressed in NAFTA. In short, U.S. telecommunication or basic communication service suppliers continued to face barriers when trying to export to the Mexican market, even with NAFTA in place.

Former Mexican President Enrique Pena Nieto enacted reforms to the country's telecommunications sector, which would allow for more foreign investment and competition in general. In addition to internal reforms to the telecommunications sector, the USMCA's telecommunications chapter (Chapter 18) has expanded and improved the NAFTA telecommunications chapter (Chapter 13). The USMCA includes general restrictions on anti-competitive practices and discriminatory practices favoring services supplied by state-owned enterprises. As a result of the USMCA, it should be easier for telecommunication service providers from Canada and the United States to access the telecommunications industry in Mexico, which reached US$23 billion (CIU 2020).

Sticking with Mexico, the emphasis on the state of the larger economy is important. For instance, the real GDP of Mexico is expected to show a greater decrease than original forecasts for the 2019–2020 period. Now, as a result of COVID-19, the IMF estimates that the Mexican economy would contract by 6.6% (Schlumbohm et al. 2020). Mexico's fiscal deficit reached 1.6% of GDP in 2018 (ibid.). The unemployment rate was 3.3% in 2019 and is projected to decline slightly to 3.2% in 2025 (ibid.).

On a more specific level with regard to the economy, it would be useful to incorporate the microeconomic trends in a specific industry within the services sector to fully understand the longevity and future prospects for growth and rapid growth. This can be done with existing publicly available statistical databases, which are created by the United Nations, the World Trade Organization, and the International Trade Centre. Taking this approach with Mexico, one may first want to know which are the top services to the Mexican market for consideration for export and investment.

Although transport services have the highest dollar value in the Mexican market, its growth rate is not the highest compared to some of the other top services imports into the Mexican market. Insurance and pension services showed the largest amount of growth at 41%, followed by financial services, 30%, from 2015 to 2019. These two industries also showed the fastest average growth rates per year—10% and 9%, respectively. During the same period, travel services experienced a 2% decline and showed negative growth rates per annum. The more detailed analysis of statistical data allows for a more thorough, focused, and accurate approach during the strategy development phase when trying to identify a service.

When analyzing statistics, it is important to look for steady growth in those top markets over the available period of time for your particular type of service. For example, a financial services provider from the United States may find that the top five export markets are the European Union, British Indian Ocean Territory, United Kingdom, Canada, and China. The top growth markets during the time frame available via Trade Map (2014–2017) are China at 33% and the United Kingdom, 13%. Access to up-to-date or real-time information is not available via this specific resource. Nevertheless, Trade Map helps service providers to follow trends to see where there has been growth in top markets for their particular service (Table 6.2).

There are limitations to the use of the statistical databases. These statistics do not cover the volatility and unpredictability of international trade, which may alter whether the top growth export market may be the most suitable for a firm. Some examples of shifts in international trade include the U.S.–China trade war, the first phase of a U.S.–China trade deal, the withdrawal of the United Kingdom from the European Union, and U.S.–UK trade talks.

Finally, the cost of doing business in a market as a result of regulatory and other micro-economic policies become important to a business owner looking to expand overseas. A simple, free tool is available from the World Bank, which is the online *Doing Business Survey* annual publication accessible at www.doingbusiness.org. This helpful resource offers an overall

Table 6.2 List of Importing Markets for Financial Services Exported by the United States of America (US$thousand)

Importers	2014	2015	2016	2017	2018
World	$106,949,000	$102,435,000	$99,384,000	$109,642,000	$113,044,000
European Union (EU 28)	$31,629,000	$30,740,000	$30,804,000	$34,699,000	n.a.
British Indian Ocean Territory	$35,468,000	$33,227,000	$28,870,000	$31,277,000	n.a.
United Kingdom	$14,539,000	$14,095,000	$14,521,000	$16,382,000	n.a.
Canada	$6,554,000	$6,039,000	$6,442,000	$6,964,000	n.a.
China	$2,953,000	$3,024,000	$3,313,000	$3,934,000	n.a.

Source: International Trade Centre Trade Map

ranking for the country that ranges from 1 to 190, which reflects the total number of economies as a part of the survey. The lower the number, the higher the ease of doing business in any given economy. As a result, that economy may be more competitive in terms of attracting trade and investment. A company would want to understand the specific rankings per different indicators to determine whether it has the resources, etc. to operate in a market that may be easy or difficult for business. The World Bank *Doing Business Survey* serves as a starting point for understanding the business environment in a country.

For instance, in the Middle East, Saudi Arabia was among the countries that showed significant improvement in terms of its ease of doing business. Saudi Arabia is a high-income country with 33.7 million people and a gross national income (GNI) per capita of US$21,540. Its 2020 rank was 62, up from 92 a year earlier. Saudi Arabia's score was 71.6 in 2020 compared to 80.07 in 2019. The World Bank report indicates that the country continued to implement reforms in key areas such as the protection of minority investors, reducing the cost of cross-border trade, and enforcing contracts, among other indicators.

U.S. companies do export services to Saudi Arabia. According to the USTR, U.S. firms exported a total of about US$9.1 billion to and imported US$1.6 billion of services from Saudi Arabia in 2018. As a result, the United States has a surplus of US$7.5 billion in its services trade with Saudi Arabia. The top U.S. services exports to Saudi Arabia include travel, professional and management services, and maintenance and repair. Services sales to Saudi Arabia are by majority U.S.-owned affiliate (U.S. Trade Representatives, Saudi Arabia).

The economic freedom index by the Heritage Foundation, a Washington, D.C.-based non-profit think tank, is another resource that is useful during the early stages of the research process, especially for microenterprises and small firms. The Heritage Foundation's annual Index of Economic Freedom measures the level of economic freedom along specific indicators which include, among others, business, trade, monetary, investment, and financial freedoms. The scores range from 0 to 100 with the latter representing economic freedom.

Sociocultural. This specific component emphasizes the decision-making and behavioral characteristics of the target consumer or client in a specific market. In other words, a sound analysis will offer focused research on the target demographic to better develop a strategy aimed toward that market. For instance, as the number one importer of U.S. services and currently engaged in trade talks with the United States, the United Kingdom may be an option for exporting a service. With the rapid global change due to the unexpected health pandemic that continued throughout the year 2020, one must have access to data that reflects current and quick changes, as well as the longer-term trends. For instance, a McKinsey and Company survey showed that European consumers, along with those from the United States and throughout most of Asia, had a far less optimistic view of economic recovery (Arora et al. 2020). The United Kingdom had an optimism level close to –10% on April 5. By June 21, that level declined further to –15%. The decreasing confidence in the economy has had an impact on consumer behavior, which, in turn, will have an impact on service suppliers. In the same McKinsey study, 44% of respondents in the United Kingdom indicated that they were "becoming more mindful of where I spend my money." Some of the areas that were identified where consumers would spend less were in the services industry, for example, food, pet care, fitness and wellness, personal care, travel, and hospitality, as discussed earlier in the chapter. Having said that, the use of online, digital shopping services continues to see steady growth in the United Kingdom. Understanding consumer behavior under different time frames and conditions allows one to make an informed decision regarding which markets may be suitable for a service.

Cultural variables are also important factors that may impact a company's performance in any given market. Visiting a country is the best way to experience and learn about a culture. Nevertheless, there are resources that are used by both scholars and practitioners in terms of comprehending the culture of a particular country or region. These approaches emphasize individual communication styles, the values that motivate individuals, and the link between societal culture and organizational cultures.

Countries with specific communication styles have been grouped into two cultural categories: low context and high context. Low context refers to those cultures where information is communicated in a direct and explicit manner. The United States, Canada, and Germany exemplify a low context culture. A high context culture is the opposite, in which communication is subtle and implicit. Non-verbal cues are important in high context cultures. Examples of countries with a high-context culture are Japan and Brazil.

Several other variables, such as individualism versus collectivism, have emerged that focus on how values shape individual behavior, motivation, and organizational culture. Being aware of the cultural context within which a service is being provided will have an impact on cross-cultural communication during negotiations and/or when collaborating with partners, etc. in the international market.

Technological. The technological factors refer to the availability of different technologies that can impact a company's ability to do business in any given overseas market. The development of a country's technology or lack thereof may present both opportunities and challenges for a service-provider, depending on the specific industry. Caribbean countries, such as the island of St. Vincent and the Grenadines, illustrate the role of technology.

St. Vincent and the Grenadines (SVG) is a Southern Caribbean country composed of the main island of St. Vincent and 32 smaller islands. The latest GDP per capita reported for the country was US$7,033.58 in 2016. The use of the internet has fluctuated dramatically within an eight-year period (2010–2018) alone in SVG. The number of people using the internet increased from 33.7% in 2010 to 47.4% in 2014. A year later, that percentage dropped dramatically to 17.13% and has slowly risen back to 22.39% in 2018 (ITU 2019). This is important to know when providing a service that requires the use of the internet, unless your service is to increase access to the internet and narrow the digital gap.

Environmental. The environmental component of the analysis focuses on the physical environment, which may have an impact on a services-based business' operations and/or revenue. In the cases of products and foods manufacturers, as well as agricultural producers, the impact of their production processes on the environment must be taken into account and/or how the existing ecological system may impact their ability to produce in a specific country. In the tertiary services sector, the development of intangible services, which adds value solely based on experience versus what a consumer can also see or touch. Nevertheless, the state of the physical environment may be more important to some services-based firms than others. For instance, there are services-based companies, as in the area of waste management, that are focused on improving the environment and environmental practices and techniques globally. Such companies will have to conduct an in-depth assessment of the physical ecological system.

Step #3: Trade Facilitation and Capacity Building

Upon assessing your firm's health and well-being to begin running the marathon toward the finish line of successfully entering an overseas market, it is important to make any lifestyle changes required to improve the health to be successful and competitive. That is where a company must develop a process by which it can export a service efficiently, while minimizing the risks as much as possible. Furthermore, it must strengthen its ability to export a service in areas such as increased capital flow and putting together a team with the right knowledge and skills.

Many government organizations at the national and domestic levels fund TFCB projects to assist countries and their local businesses with the technical assistance necessary to help local firms export to the global market. There are a number of state and local initiatives that use funding from the National Export Initiative (NEI) to provide workshops, training, and business match-making and trade shows and trade missions to facilitate the international trade process and make it easier for the business owner. The NEI was announced by former U.S. President Barack Obama in his 2010 State of the Union address. The goal was to double U.S. exports within a five-year period. Furthermore, during the Obama administration, U.S. government assistance was enhanced to assist the SMEs through technical assistance and financing and networking. As a part of the initiative, an effort was placed on promoting exports in the service sector, which represented close to 30% of total U.S. exports (U.S. Department of State 2017).

Different states that receive federal funding use that money to assist businesses throughout the state. For instance, the state of California, through the Governor's Office of Business and Economic Development (GO-Biz), uses funds from the U.S. Small Business Administration (SBA) as a part of its California State Trade Expansion Program (STEP). Through collaboration with the local SBA offices and the local chapters of the California International Trade and Development (CITD) offices services are provided to assist local first-time exporters. Also, the SBA district office for Orange County and the Inland Empire and the California Center for International Trade and Development (Inland Empire), the latter of which by the time of this writing is no longer operating, collaborated to provide workshops to businesses that were new to the idea of exporters and/or were first-time exporters via the Export Trade Assistance Program (ETAP). One should check with the local SBA office to see what types of programs exist at the city and state-levels to help with exports, and particularly services exports, to the overseas market. Upon completing the research on the market, take advantage of the programs that can provide additional resources to specific markets that, again, will make it easier than going it alone.

Assess whether your firm is healthy enough to enter one market over another. That is where the capacity building comes in. Upon doing a diagnostic assessment of your firm's health for global expansion, select the market for which your firm has the capacity to export. That means getting access to capital, hiring the right expertise, etc. to ensure that not only is the market right for your service, but that your capability to deliver that service is right for that market.

Step #4: Develop a Strategy Appropriate for Your Business and the Export Market

One of the things that is suggested is fully understanding the options for strategy and evaluate the best strategy development to understand *why* one is doing something versus just the *what* and *how*. There are different strategies that companies are encouraged to consider, such as Michael Porter's competitive advantage model, which is "the creation of a unique and valuable position, involving a different set of activities" (Porter 2011, 16). In other words, Porter's model goes beyond just low cost but also quality, industry clusters, firm strategy, and government role.

Another useful strategy would be to see if your service could be provided in a new marketplace and, thus, create a new demand. In this case, competition initially would not be such a huge factor, since you are presenting something completely new and creating a demand (for more, see Kim and Mauborgne 2004). This is possible in untapped, overlooked markets. One observation is that many companies, especially the small companies that are just learning how to export, want to go to the larger, saturated markets just because they hear more about them, for example, China and Brazil. However, they do not consider the stiff competition not just from other companies from the United States but from all around the world. As a result, they overlook the enormous amount of opportunities in other larger or even smaller economies that may not have the types of services that they may provide but can do so while strategically and effectively creating a demand for their service. That still requires understanding the market and the target audience, not blindly going in with passion about a service and expecting it to succeed. Otherwise, you are in a sea of competition and price becomes the determining factor for the ability to compete, which may not bode very well for a services-based firm.

Just as with training for a marathon, it is wise to know why you are engaging in certain practices. In other words, beyond running, training regularly, and eating well, you need to know what different strategies or approaches may work. For example, during a conversation with a student studying international trade, the student mentioned that these strategies learned allowed him to go back to his employer and explain why a certain strategy would work over another to improve their export success.

CASE STUDY 6.1 INSIGHTS ON RESEARCH PRIOR TO SELLING TO A FOREIGN MARKET

"It's incredibly important to incorporate that research component when you are starting to think about an export program ... to understand, first of all, where the best opportunities for your products or services [are] .... How would you know that if you just are guessing?"

Devorah Kaufman, Senior Account Manager, Euromonitor International

---

Euromonitor International is a research company that provides strategic market research, data, and analyses on countries, producers, and services worldwide. Organizations can use their information to expand overseas or help their clients or members to leverage international business opportunities. Senior Account Manager for Euromonitor International, Devorah Kaufman, who is based in Chicago, IL, offers insight into why research is important and tips that small and medium-sized companies can use prior to starting the export process.

The research as a part of a company's export program should answer basic questions: Who? What? Where? Why? How? Getting answers to these questions will help a company identify the best market opportunities for its products or services, according to Ms. Kaufman.

Just going after a market because it has a large, growing population without doing in-depth research may prove inadequate for a company's export strategy. Using China as an example, Ms. Kaufman explains:

> A lot of times, people say I want to do business in China, because China has one billion people, and if I sell one of my products to one tenth of one percent of the population, then I'll be a zillionaire. But China might not be the best opportunity. That market might be saturated in China. It might be hard to find a distributor in China. The market might not be growing in China. So, you want to understand which markets around the world have the best opportunities

for your particular product or service. Sometimes that's looking at the current and forecast market sales or market size for [the] product or service. Sometimes it's looking at demographic trends or population or government, things that are happening in the market to understand where the market could be going.

Once a company has answered the basic questions, as suggested above, the next step is to rank the countries by their market potential for the company's product or service. Looking at the top three to five countries with such a market potential is a good start to identifying the right market.

To determine the number one market for exporting, an analysis of the business environment in each of the three to five countries with market potential will be required.

You want to understand the conditions within those markets ... how to do business in those markets, where are the major population centers, or where are the best opportunities within those countries. Are there corruption or other types of issues in those countries? What are the trends of those countries? Because if you're making a product or service here [in the United States], you might need to tweak it for that [country], and usually you do.

Understanding the specific consumer preferences is another key component of adequately analyzing the market in another country.

E-commerce continues to make it easier for a company to make a sale to consumers outside of its domestic market online. What may appear as an easy market may actually result in a company overlooking the market with greater potential and that offers far greater and easier access, as Ms. Kaufman reveals.

Sometimes when small businesses are just getting started with exporting ... they have a website [and] they might get some sales online.... So, let's say that they got a sale from somebody in China, and they go, oh wow, we can do a lot of business in China. Really, if they'd sit down and do their research, they might find that some place like Mexico, [with] which we share our border [and] we have trade agreements. It might be much easier to get started and there's a much bigger opportunity in those nearby countries like Canada and Mexico.

Just because you got a sale online doesn't mean that's representative of the market; and definitely, you want to investigate that opportunity if you're going to be spending your time and energy. You want to spend that on the places that have the best potential, which are going to give you the most bang for your buck. And so that's where you have to do some research and try and narrow down and understand those markets, which you are going to target.

CASE STUDY 6.2 PROVIDING CONSULTING SERVICES OVERSEAS

"If you don't understand the market and you don't understand the culture and you don't understand the rule of law, you are really putting yourself and the success of whatever enterprise you want to put in that country at risk."

Jim Gitney, CEO, Group 50

Group 50 is a Southern Californian consulting firm founded in 2004 and that focuses on three practice areas: business strategy, talent strategy, and operational execution. The firm provides services to companies generating anywhere between US$50 million and US$1 billion annually, many of which are U.S. companies that set up operations overseas. Group 50 also provides consulting services for companies that are looking to operate in the U.S. market. That may entail helping the company create its supply chain and structuring its sales force and business development activities in the U.S. market. In other words, Group 50 serves as the in-country partner to a foreign company that wants to introduce its product to the U.S. market. Group 50 CEO Jim Gitney estimates that between 15% and 20% of the company's revenue comes from providing a service to foreign companies.

Mr. Gitney shares information about the firm's services and important lessons that he has learned from his own experience with exporting Group 50's services.

As Mr. Gitney explains:

Almost all of your work is structured around the supply chain.... The global supply chain has gotten very complex and is becoming more and more of an issue in validating the integrity of the materials you're getting. Does it meet the product requirements? Does it meet the contractual requirements?

Blockchain technology is one of the types of technologies that is being incorporated into the supply chain. Group 50 advises companies on how technology can improve the efficiency of their supply chains, as Mr. Gitney discusses further:

> When we work with global companies, our focus is on helping them leverage technology to make their supply chain more efficient and more robust and more resilient. Blockchain is an element that allows the use of technology to automate a lot of things that typically [have] been done by hand in the past, such as validating the quantity of goods that came in and allowing a smart contract to release payments to the vendor.... And so blockchain is really just another element of all of the technologies that are used to manage the global supply chain.

So how does Group 50 even reach clients internationally? "Seventy percent of my business comes from [an] organic search on the internet," says Mr. Gitney. The company has a team of people that help with its SEO strategy and generating content-related supply chain.

In addition to internet searches, the network developed by Mr. Gitney and other members of the Group 50 team has helped in terms of securing international business projects. That network comes from many years working for a corporate firm, establishing connections, and building relationships. The Group 50 CEO adds, "So when you're starting up a consulting firm after leaving corporate America, you have a pretty robust rolodex, and the acquisition of projects is easier, because you also have a very well-documented and defined skill set."

In 2020, Group 50 worked on projects for two separate Canadian companies. Although Group 50's journey includes lessons throughout, one experience with an effort to secure a deal with a large agriculture-based company in Saudi Arabia in 2019 was shared to highlight key things that a firm should consider when working with a foreign company:

1. Culture: Gain a solid comprehension of the culture in a country and how business is done in that country.
2. Rule of law: Understand the rule of law in the country, since U.S. rule of law varies from that found in a country such as Saudi Arabia. Hiring an attorney who understands contracts in that country is important.
3. Language: Whereas language differences are a given, it is also important to understand the context. On this specific item, Mr. Gitney says,

"Because there is a language dynamic, you have to be incredibly careful about what you thought you heard."

4. Payment: When doing business in foreign market, it is important to make sure that contracts are arranged in a way to ensure payment for any work completed.

Whereas identifying a need is one way to select a market for one's service, Mr. Gitney adds a slightly different take on this approach. "What you do may be needed, but it's really important to understand: What is the required form for it to be delivered or provided? There is a difference between the two, because delivered is more product focused, and provided is more service focused."

Bibliography

Aleman, Sergio E. 2001. "NAFTA and its impact on the privatization of Mexico's telecommunications industry." *Law and Business Review of the Americas* 7 (1):5–16.

Arora, Nidhi; Tamara Charm; Anne Grimmelt; Mianne Ortega et al. 2020. "Consumer sentiment and behavior continue to reflect the uncertainty of the COVID-19 crisis." *McKinsey and Company*. July 8, 2020.

Beckerman, Michael. 2020. "Passing USMCA will help U.S. companies address global threats to digital trade." June 10. https://thehill.com/blogs/congress-blog/politics/477741-passing-usmca-will-help-us-companies-address-global-threats-to.

Chander, Anupam. 2018. "The coming North American digital trade zone." October 9. https://www.cfr.org/blog/coming-north-american-digital-trade-zone.

CIU. "Telecommunication revenue in Mexico in 2020, by segment (in billion Mexican pesos)." Graph. January 1, 2020. Statista. Accessed September 26, 2020. https://www-statista-com.ezproxy.snhu.edu/statistics/722621/telecommunication-revenue-segment-distribution-mexico/.

Harrison, Kate. 2015. "What's different about business overseas? One map says it all." *Forbes Magazine*, February 25.

Heimann, Fritz F. 1997. "Combatting international corruption: The role of the business community." In *Corruption and the Global Economy*, edited by Kimberly Ann Elliott, 147–61. Washington, DC: Peterson Institute for International Economics.

ICC (International Chamber of Commerce). n.d. "Combatting corruption." https://iccwbo.org/global-issues-trends/responsible-business/combatting-corruption/.

IMF. October 11, 2019. "St. Vincent and the Grenadines: Gross domestic product (GDP) per capita in current prices from 1984 to 2024 (in U.S. dollars)." Chart. Statista. Accessed September 30, 2020. https://www-statista-com.ezproxy.snhu

.edu/statistics/731145/gross-domestic-pro duct-gdp-per-capita-in-st-vincent-and
-the-grenadines/.

International Trade Centre. n.d. *Trade Map.* Accessed September 30, 2020. Geneva:
International Trade Centre. https://www.trademap.org/.

ITU. July 24, 2019. "Percentage of population using the internet in Saint Vincent
and the Grenadines from 2010 to 2018." Chart. Statista. Accessed September
30, 2020. https://www-statista-com.ezproxy.snhu.edu/statistics/1055511/inte
rnet-penetration-saint-vincent-grenadines/.

Kim, W. Chan; and Renee Mauborgne. 2004. "Blue ocean strategy." *Harvard
Business Review.* Accessed September 28, 2020. https://hbr.org/2004/10/blue-o
cean-strategy.

Matthews, Barbara C. 2019. "How the USMCA impacts transatlantic trade policy."
https://www.atlanticcouncil.org/blogs/new-atlanticist/how-the-usmca-impacts
-transatlantic-trade-policy/.

Schlumbohm, Maike; Volker Staffa; Maike Zeppernick; and Joline Franken.
"Mexico: Statista country report." 2020. *Statista,* June 2020.

Porter, Michael E. 2011. What is strategy? In *HBR's 10 Must Reads on Strategy
(Including Featured Article 'What Is Strategy?' by Michael E. Porter).* Boston,
MA: Harvard Business Review Press.

Rampell, Catherine. 2020. "Even with the administration's about face on international student visas, enrollment is still set to plummet." Washington Post. https
://www.washingtonpost.com/opinions/2020/07/14/even-with-administrations
-about-face-international-student-visas-enrollment-is-still-set-plummet/.

Rosenbaum, Eric. 2019. You'll be shocked to learn how many small businesses still
don't have a website. Accessed September 23, 2020. https://www.cnbc.com
/2017/06/14/tech-help-wanted-about-half-of-small-businesses-dont-have-a-web
site.html.

US-China Business Council. n.d. "2020 state export report." Accessed September
30, 2020. https://www.uschina.org/reports/2020-state-export-report.

U.S. Department of State. 2017. "The National Export Initiative: Stimulating Global
Economic Growth Through U.S. Exports." Accessed September 30, 2020. https
://2009-2017.state.gov/r/pa/scp/fs/2010/134811.htm.

USTR (United States Trade Representative). 2019. "National trade estimate report on
foreign trade barriers." Accessed September 30, 2020. https://ustr.gov/sites/de
fault/files/2019_National_Trade_Estimate_Report.pdf.

USTR. n.d.a. "Saudi Arabia." Accessed September 28. https://ustr.gov/countries-reg
ions/europe-middle-east/middle-eastnorth-africa/saudi-arabia#:~:text=Trade%2
0Balance,%2C%20down%206.9%25%20from%202017.

USTR. n.d.b. "United States: Mexico: Canada trade fact sheet modernizing NAFTA
into a 21st century trade agreement." Accessed September 24, 2020. https://us
tr.gov/trade-agreements/free-trade-agreements/united-states-mexico-canada-a
greement/fact-sheets/modernizing.

World Economic Forum. n.d. Network of Global Agenda Councils Reports 2011–
2012: Anti-Corruption. Accessed on September 30, 2020. https://reports.wefo
rum.org/global-agenda-council-2012/councils/anti-corruption/.

"Worldwide Governance Indicators." n.d. World Bank. https://info.worldbank.org/governance/wgi/Home/Reports.

Wu, Mark. 2017. *Digital Trade-Related Provisions in Regional Trade Agreements: Existing Models and Lessons for the Multilateral Trade System*, edited by RTA Exchange. Geneva: International Centre for Trade and Sustainable Development (ICTSD) Inter-American Development Bank (IDB).

Chapter 7

Using Grants and Contracts to Export a Service

A common concern among consultants and advisors to firms, particularly small-sized firms, is that their clients lack the money to move forward in the international market and do not know how to secure a grant or contract to assist in their efforts to export a service, as well as a good, to the overseas market. These concerns are addressed in this chapter through a detailed description of how to find the grant and contract opportunities, what the grant and contract processes include, and what to consider when putting together a grant or contract proposal. The case study toward the end of the chapter illustrates why the grant and contract opportunities are important to service providers and how to navigate and succeed in the process.

The grants and contract process benefits firms of all sizes, because the process is transparent, ensures payment, and helps to reduce risks. Although the process of applying for grants and contracts may be considered time-consuming, especially for small firms with limited resources, that time pales in comparison to navigating the market alone; trying to build a trustworthy, qualified network of people; and facing a higher risk of lost time and money only to possibly not achieve the desired results.

Finding Grants and Contracts

The United States has several federal government agencies that offer grants, which provide the funds needed to carry out an idea and proposed project.

The service-provider does not have to worry about paying these funds back. Nevertheless, the service-provider must keep in mind that any proposed project has to offer community-wide benefit such as one that creates jobs, boosts productivity, enhances safety, increases revenue for local businesses, or contributes to economic development. These grants can be located at the free website, www.grants.gov, which serves as a one-stop shop for finding U.S. federally funded grants from agencies such as the U.S. Agency for International Development (USAID), the Millennium Challenge Corporation (MCC), and the U.S. Department of State (DOS). Registration is required with Grants.gov. The grants can be searched based along the following criteria:

- Status of the grants: Interested parties can search for grants that are current, forthcoming, and closed grants.
- Eligibility: Grants can be searched based on those for the larger for-profit organizations, small businesses, and individuals, among other categories.
- Category: A grant can be found related to an exporter's area of interest and expertise such as agriculture, business and commerce, and energy.
- Agency: An exporter can look at a specific agency for relevant grants. For example, in addition to the agencies previously listed, other agencies may include the U.S. Department of Agriculture (USDA) and the U.S. Department of Energy (DOE).

For fiscal year 2020, the U.S. federal agencies combined spent US$7.2 trillion ("COVID-19 Spending Data"). Of that total spending amount, 71%, or US$5.1 trillion, went to grants and fixed charges. With regard to specific budget areas, international affairs accounted for 0.9%, or US$63 billion, of the total U.S. federal government spending. Agriculture represented 0.3%, or US$24 billion; and Energy, 0.2% or US$14.1 billion ("COVID-19 Spending Data").

The contract process refers to the procurement of services by an agency that will help that same agency in its efforts through coordinated projects. A service provider would have to respond to an announcement regarding the project designed by the agency and bid on that project. Both U.S.- and non-U.S.-based service-providers can include contracts offered by federal agencies mentioned earlier as a part of their export strategy. The procurement opportunities have also been placed on the Grants.gov website. In order to take advantage of the opportunities on the Grants.gov website and do business with the U.S. government, a firm, whether U.S. or non-U.S.-based, must also register with the System for Award Management (SAM) website (https://

sam.gov/SAM). SAM is operated by the U.S. General Services Administration, a Washington, D.C.-based independent agency created to assist with the management of and basic-level function of federal agencies. SAM itself "collects, validates, stores, and disseminates business information about the federal government's trading partners in support of the contract awards, grants, and electronic payment processes" (Grants.gov). A Data Universal Numbering System (DUNS) number for a business entity and a Taxpayer Identification Number (TIN) or Employer Identification Number (EIN) are required for registration. Upon registration, the service-provider will be able to take advantage of the numerous contract opportunities with the U.S. government at all levels—federal, state, and local.

Additionally, service-providers internationally can seek the contract opportunities presented by multilateral development banks (MDBs) such as the World Bank, Inter-American Development Bank (IDB), African Development Bank (AfDB), and the Asian Development Bank (ADB). Many of these opportunities can be found on the United Nations Development Business (UNDB) website at https://devbusiness.un.org/. The UNDB also posts contracts for United Nations' agencies, for example, UN Development Programme (UNDP); UN Educational, Scientific, and Cultural Organization (UNESCO); and UN Environment Programme (UNEP). The UNDB online platform also includes a list of other organizations and institutions that procure services. According to the UNDB website, the UNDB is a global network that offers access to information about contracts in more than 180 countries worldwide and from 19 business sectors. The UNDB is subscription-based, even though it does offer very limited complimentary access to information. A one-year full subscription offers individual access to procurement notices, consultancy projects for firms and individuals, and contract awards, among other data and services. A corporate subscription includes five individual accounts with access to information about contract opportunities, etc.

Another resource for finding contracts and participating in the procurement process, which is also fee-based, is Devex. Devex defines itself as "[t]he media platform for the global development community." An individual service-provider can use Devex to find funding organized by the time frame; sector, including the services sector; monetary value of the projects; and status of the project (e.g. opened, closed, or canceled). (Notably, Devex also lists grant opportunities.) Furthermore, an individual consultant or organization seeking increased visibility has the option of creating a profile highlighting his/her expertise and experience so that this information can appear in searches for other potential partners for any given project. Devex, similar to UNDP, allows one to register and take advantage of its complimentary and limited access. To gain greater access, Devex offers two subscription plans, which are mentioned publicly on the website. Individual service-providers gain access to news, in-depth analyses, events, and its job board for the less expensive plan. The second plan provides access to funding opportunities from more than 850 sources, as well as news, in-depth analyses, events, etc.

The UNDP and Devex offer a central location to track contract opportunities with the MDBs, as well as alerts that are sent out when those opportunities become available. For complimentary access to the announcements that are published, one can go directly to the website of the agency of interest. For example, the IDB announces procurement opportunities throughout Latin America and the Caribbean for various sectors on its website. According to the IDB website, between 20,000 and 30,000 contracts are generated annually for eligible firms and individuals that provide consulting services, as well as goods and works. To be eligible, an organization must come from an IDB member country. The procurement process at the corporate level consists of the buying of services, as well as goods, that satisfy the internal needs of the organization. The procurement notices for the IDB include a detailed description about the project, the process of submitting a project bid, and the appropriate contact person(s) for the project.

Procurement Process

Project announcement or solicitation. Each agency will publish a description of the overseas project. These announcements are referred to as tenders, which invite eligible firms and individuals to submit a bid for a project. In some cases, a procurement notice may first just include a general overview of the project and require firms to submit an Expression of Interest (EOI), which is then used by the agency to create a shortlist of companies or individuals to send a Request for Proposal (RFP), or the full announcement. (The announcement may take on other names such as Annual Program Statement (APS), Broad Agency Announcement (BAA), or Notice of Funding Opportunity (NFO).) The RFP will include the Terms of Reference (TOR) for the project and contract, as well as instructions and due dates for submitting a contract proposal. The TOR consists of information such as the project background, context, objectives, services to be rendered, payment, etc.

Technical proposal submission. Proposal consists of basic information across the board that will be shared here. However, any company or individual interested in the cross-border export of a service should still review each agency's requirement for the structure, etc. of the proposal prior to submission. Overall, a competitive proposal effectively emphasizes expertise, experience, past results, proposed approach, and expected results to adequately address the problem highlighted in the RFP.

Proposal review. The funding agency will review the proposal, per the criteria used to determine the final recipient of the award. The criteria that the agency uses and the weight of each criteria (e.g. past performance, technical approach, and the organization's capabilities) toward the final decision may be included in the announcement.

Award decision. Upon a review of the proposals that have been submitted, per the guidelines laid out in the RFP and TOR, the funding agency will notify the organizations of their final decision. For U.S. federal contracts, the website USAspending.gov includes the recipient (prime and subcontractor) of the award, the final dollar amount, length of the project, and the awarding agency.

Putting Together the Expression of Interest

The EOI is a mini proposal in response to a tender that shows that a company is interested in bidding on a project and is eligible and qualified to do so. As stated above, the awarding agency will create a shortlist of firms to submit a full proposal. The EOI, generally speaking, consists of several pieces of information listed below. The details for each piece of information are suggestions based on my first-hand experience writing successful EOIs for projects funded by MDBs.

Cover letter. The recommended length for the cover letter is one page that expresses interest in the specific project in a concise manner. Next, a brief statement about the company and broad relevant experience (e.g. having worked on federally funded projects, expertise in the subject matter). This information can be followed by direct relevant experience that demonstrates, for instance, knowledge of the region or specific country and experience with working on projects regardless of region with the same objectives. Finally, the letter can end with a statement about the possibility of drafting a technical proposal to meet the agency's needs.

Table of Contents. The cover letter is usually followed by a Table of Contents that includes sections such as the Introduction, Project Context, Expertise, Corporate Qualifications/Capabilities, and the Team.

Introduction. The Introduction, once again, highlights the firm's interest in the specific project and its direct past and current relevant experience. Then, this section lays out the organization of the EOI itself.

Project context. Being a firm with a team equipped with in-depth knowledge about the subject matter and/or knows how to complete substantive, accurate market research is helpful toward drafting the Project Context section. This section discusses the project and its significance. For example, one project announcement focused on enhancing the capacity for the export of goods from Caribbean countries intra- and extra-regionally. The EOI placed this information within the situation at the time of the Caribbean countries awaiting full implementation of the Caribbean Single Market Economy (CSME) and when many lost duty-free access to the EU market when the EU's preferential access to African, Caribbean, and Pacific (ACP) countries was ruled a violation of the WTO Agreement on Trade in Goods. With these impactful events, the EOI discussed how the firm would assist the region in facilitating trade and enhancing their capacity to export to new markets starting at the national level.

Expertise. The section lists the areas of expertise of the team members relevant to the project announcement. For a more competitive EOI, the information should go beyond just a laundry list of knowledge areas but also incorporate brief statements highlighting results of that expertise on a similar project or various projects.

Corporate qualifications. This section emphasizes the projects on which the firm has worked either as a prime contractor or subcontractor. For a firm just getting started, partnerships and collaborations with other businesses that may bring additional qualifications to the final proposal are essential.

Team and curriculum vitae. In addition to including the curriculum vitae, the section focuses on the strength of the team member, how that team member will contribute to the success of the project based on past performances, and the team member's educational background. The description or short bio following the name of each team member should be no more than one paragraph and aligned with the requirements of the project. At the same time, the bio should not be a long run-on paragraph or several paragraphs that just list a series of degrees, certificates, awards, and association memberships. Considering that the competition may also include a team with varying levels of accomplishments, the expertise, skills, and performance help to strengthen the proposal.

The Components of the Technical Proposal

The technical proposal is submitted when a firm decides to or is invited to bid on a tender. The proposal itself has different components that require a well-thought-out, strategic approach to increase one's chance of winning an award.

Cover letter and letters of commitment. The cover letter is an important part of the proposal and should not be taken lightly. The cover letter expresses interest in the project and provides a brief introduction of the type of service that will be provided and the way in which it will be provided for the benefit of the end users in the overseas country. The next would be to include firms leading the project and the relevant expertise of the team joining the project, which, again, goes beyond academic accomplishments toward practical results. Letters of commitment drafted and signed by each partnering firm are also included in the final proposal submission. Following the cover letter and letters of commitment can be a page with a list of acronyms and the Table of Contents.

Executive summary. The executive summary outlines the key points of the proposal, for which the details are provided in the technical section.

Technical approach. The technical approach may include several sections designed to demonstrate adequate understanding of the problem based on primary and secondary research, the organization's approach to addressing the problem, the methodology behind the approach, how the team will implement specific tasks and activities, how success will be measured, and why the team is most appropriate for the project. The curriculum vitae or resume for each team member should be included at the end of the proposal. The key thing to remember is that the proposal should show that the firm and its partners have the resources to implement the strategies proposed over the course of the project, especially those that are multiyear projects.

Budget narrative. Although keeping costs low is important, it is also noteworthy that the budget proposal is feasible in an effort to provide a quality service and produce results. In other words, it may not always be the lowest cost proposal that results in being awarded a contract. The budget includes an overview of the following:

■ Salaries of the staff on the project such as the project lead or program manager, country director, financial officer;
■ Salaries for local staff to assist with the project such as a project accountant;

- Fringe benefits for all staff included;
- Payment to contractors (e.g. consultants);
- Direct costs (space rental, office supplies, office equipment, utilities, communication systems, security);
- Indirect costs;
- Other costs (e.g. air travel and local transport, housing per diem, meals and incidental expenses (M&IE), costs of any materials and their transport, danger pay).

Recommendations

The process also includes other related activities beyond drafting a technical proposal in response to an RFP and awaiting the final award decision that would enhance the competitive edge of a firm during the process.

Networking. Sometimes when tenders are posted, there may be only one month to submit a final bid. By establishing a strong network of connections with representatives from the various government agencies and MDBs mentioned here, one may get a head start by gaining additional insight into any possible upcoming projects, additional insight into the agency's funding priorities, and suggestions for submitting a competitive bid. These same connections may be useful even after an award has been given. For instance, when it comes to an unsuccessful grant application, an agency representative may offer feedback that can be applied toward a future grant application.

Furthermore, networking strategically and consistently serves as a great asset when having to put together a qualified team for the implementation phase of the project.

Market research. By traveling to a country or visiting virtually, as the increase in the use of digital services allows for distant-level connections, a consultant can make additional connections and collect useful data that can be applied toward a feasible and reasonable technical proposal.

Attend training sessions offered by government agencies and MDBs. In addition to the information on the websites of the agencies and MDBs, they may also host special sessions to help business representatives comprehend their mission and objectives plus navigate the procurement process.

In sum, a services-based exporter, whether an individual or organization, can include grants and contacts as a part of the business model and strategy.

CASE STUDY 7.1 EXPORTING TO THE CARIBBEAN REGION THROUGH CONTRACTS

"It's about developing the relationship. Well, two things, I would say developing the expertise, showcasing the expertise, and then really developing and nurturing the relationship. For a small company, partnerships are really important."

—Andrea Ewart, Founder and CEO, DevelopTradeLaw, LLC

DevelopTradeLaw, LLC, a customs and trade law/consulting firm located in Washington, D.C., provides legal services to private clients and consulting services to governments primarily in developing and emerging markets. Many of the latter services are predominantly funded by International Financial Institutions (IFIs) and international development agencies, for example, the USAID or the European Fund. The projects that are secured through these funded contracts have allowed the firm, which began in 2003, to continue to grow and expand to overseas' markets, in this case, mainly throughout the Caribbean region, which consists of numerous small island developing states.* More specifically, exporting a service to an overseas market through these types of contracts present a steady stream of revenue over a longer period of time when compared to working on shorter-term projects, which vary, for private clients.

Whereas, DevelopTradeLaw advises business owners on the compliance regulations of which they need to be aware and offers solutions to the challenges that a company may encounter, such as getting an item stuck in customs, its consulting work with the government emphasize putting in place the infrastructure to allow for smoother international trade. When comparing the firm's foreign government consulting services to working with private clients, Ms. Ewart says that "those services are very different, although related. So, it might be anything from helping a country to understand an obligation … assisting them with implementing it, whether it is drafting legislation or developing the policy to support the process of meeting their obligations."

---

* The United Nations defines Small Island Developing States (SIDS) as a special group of developing countries from the islands of the Caribbean Sea; the Atlantic, Indian, and Pacific Oceans; and the Mediterranean and South China Seas. Countries from these geographical regions face deeper social, economic, and environmental vulnerabilities that restrict sustainable development (see United Nations 2020).

Some of these projects have been developed by the funding agencies to help countries to meet their requirements under the international trade policy framework set by the WTO Trade Facilitation Agreement (TFA). The TFA took effect on February 22, 2017, and consists of three sections designed to 1) expedite "the movement, release, and clearance of goods in transit"; 2) offer developing and least-developed countries (LDCs) the option to decide when they will implement individual provisions within the TFA upon receiving technical assistance; and 3) creating a permanent WTO-level trade facilitation committee while requiring member countries to maintain a national committee to assist with TFA implementation ("The Trade Facilitation Agreement: An overview"). So far, 153 of the 164 WTO members have accepted the Agreement. Some of the ratifying members include countries from the Caribbean region, which is where most of Ms. Ewart's consulting projects for government entities take place.

For instance, Ms. Ewart has been able to provide her expertise to Trinidad and Tobago, located in the southern Caribbean region. The dual-island country is one of the WTO members that accepted the TFA. Ms. Ewart participated in an MDB-funded project to help the Caribbean nation to comply with its commitments through the implementation of the Single Electronic Window, or Single Window (SW) system. The SW is designed to simplify the system of data submission and regulatory control by streamlining coordination efforts and requirements at the national and international levels. The World Customs Organization (WCO) uses the phrase, "Single Window Environment (SWE)" to reflect the "systemic nature of the Single Window as a network of interdependent facilities of cross-border regulatory agencies and other stakeholders." The WCO defines the SWE as "a cross border, 'intelligent', facility that allows parties involved in trade and transport to lodge standardized information, mainly electronic, with a single entry point to fulfill all import, export and transit related regulatory requirements" (World Customs Organization).

Businesses, including small firms, can gain from the adding government contracting to their export strategy, as Ms. Ewart explains.

> They provide a steady, stable income flow…. With the private sector, if you're not able to get a nice retainer client, you have to constantly [get] new clients and the work that is involved…. [For] any company that want to go into government contracting, it is difficult to get in there, but it can be very rewarding, a good additional stream, because getting a new client or even getting a repeat client,

which is the easier way to go on the private sector side, is much more challenging.

Government contracting is a part of the company's sustainable strategy— diversification. The government contracting adds to the private sector service that DevelopTradeLaw, LLC provides. Even within the government contracting space, diversification has helped the firm to engage with different types of projects. One strategy has been to look at contracts of different sizes from the different development agencies. Many of the contracts, depending on the funding agency, vary in terms of the dollar value and the length of the contract, which can range anywhere from a few months to years.

Contracts also provide an opportunity to export a service to different countries in distinctive regions worldwide. Ms. Ewart's consulting services to foreign governments is predominantly in the Caribbean region. However, as she explains, there are many other small island developing states. Additionally, Europe leads in terms of regional integration efforts, which also provides opportunities and insight into which practices are most effective. She has provided consulting services to other developing countries and emerging markets in different regions, for example, Brazil, Algeria, and Zambia.

Furthermore, the process of going after a government contract entails activities outside of the procurement steps themselves. DevelopTradeLaw, LLC continues to showcase its in-depth expertise in specific areas such as licensing, customs, regulatory compliance, and international trade law. Furthermore, as Ms. Ewart explains, establishing and nurturing long-term trustworthy relationships are key. These types of relationships become useful when learning about contracting opportunities. Tracking opportunities requires the time and money to do so, as DevelopTradeLaw, LLC has discovered. Nevertheless, relationships with other small business owners have been helpful in terms of those consultants sharing contract opportunities either to partner on the project or because it may not necessarily be a project that they would undertake but aligns with the expertise and experience of DevelopTradeLaw, LLC. Trustworthy relationships remain key to avoid sharing expertise for a contract proposal and not being included in the implementation of the project. Using these relationships to develop one's own team to put toward a project proposal has been helpful to this international trade law firm.

Finally, doing quality work and leaving a positive impression increases one's likelihood of even learning about these opportunities through direct referrals. The recent project in Trinidad and Tobago emerged from two people who referred her to a company looking for someone with her expertise. As Ms. Ewart explains, "There are referrals that come from first of all, doing a good job ... but then maintaining those connections so that you are top of mind and someone will remember you when the right opportunity comes up."

Bibliography

"COVID-19 Spending Data." n.d. https://www.usaspending.gov/.

General Services Administration. 2020. "System for Award Management." Accessed September 29, 2020. https://sam.gov/SAM/.

"Grants.gov." n.d. https://www.grants.gov/.

"The trade facilitation agreement: An overview." n.d. World Trade Organization. Accessed August 26, 2020. https://www.wto.org/english/tratop_e/tradfa_e/trad fatheagreement_e.htm.

United Nations. 2020. "About the small Island developing states." *UN of the High Representative for the Least Developed Countries, Landlocked Developing Countries and Small Island Developing States*. Accessed September 29, 2020. http://unohrlls.org/about-sids/.

World Customs Organization. n.d. Accessed September 29, 2020. http://www.wcoo md.org/en/topics/facilitation/activities-and-programmes/national-single-window /single-window.aspx.

Chapter 8

Using E-commerce and Other Digital Technologies to Reach Global Markets

During the early stages of the shelter-in-place and stay-at-home orders and guidelines in the United States in response to the coronavirus, the impact of the health crisis on e-commerce became apparent. "COVID-19 will forever change retailing, and its initial impact on e-Commerce is creating challenges to online selling and service …," writes Forbes senior contributor Louis Columbus (2020). US and Canadian e-commerce orders increased by 129% by April 21 compared to the previous year (Columbus 2020). Other findings highlight that e-commerce grew by 4–6 years in 2020 alone, as a result of the global health pandemic (Koetsier 2020). These rapid changes in buying behavior can be felt by buyers and sellers of services, as well as goods, worldwide.

Notably, not only have these changes been seen when it comes to consumer behavior. The health crisis and the increased use of e-commerce and other forms of digital platforms have forced service providers to alter their perspective surrounding e-commerce, if necessary, and develop an effective strategy that would allow them to continue to provide a service domestically and internationally in the *new global economy*. Whereas many service providers had already embraced the opportunities presented by these technologies, many had to play a game of catch-up.

The chapter helps us to first understand what e-commerce is; how it, along with other digital technologies, plays a significant role in the cross-border trade in services; and its impact on exporters' ability to compete in the global marketplace.

E-Commerce

Broadly speaking, e-commerce points to the idea of buying and selling goods and services electronically over the internet and the exchange of money to carry out these online commercial transactions. Usually, the discussion surrounding the facilitation of e-commerce emphasizes online stores through third-party platforms such as Amazon, Alibaba, E-bay, Etsy, or Shopify. These transactions occur among different parties—Business to Business (B2B), Business to Customer (B2C), Consumer to Business (C2B), and Consumer to Consumer (C2C) (Aljifri et al. 2003). However, an interview with Hema Dey, owner, president, and CEO of Iffel International, reveals that an online shopping cart is not always necessary when engaging in e-commerce, as in the case of the services sector. She says:

> E-commerce in my vocabulary stands for electronic commerce, and commerce and marketing is based on the theory of exchange when a good or service is exchanged for payment and money … To me, electronic commerce stands for that exchange and that can mean either exchange through a shopping cart, or it could also mean an exchange when you get a lead for a service that you provide. So, you don't necessarily have to have a shopping cart to be under the umbrella of e-commerce.

By 1999, the United States represented 80% of total global e-commerce (OECD 1999, 13). The United States became the leader in the e-commerce space, because it did not face the same constraints that providers in Europe and Asia faced such as high costs, the lack of sufficient bandwidth, and the slower pace of liberalization of the telecommunications sector (OECD 1999, 13). E-commerce has been made possible through the internet. Although the precursor to the internet goes as far back as the 1960s, it was the invention of the world wide web and browser during the 1990s that created the possibility for e-commerce (OECD 1999, 10). Additionally, in the United States, the liberalization of the telecommunications sector, in which the regulations were loosened to allow for more private sector competition, as well as the innovations from the private sector, resulted in the growth and evolvement of e-commerce (OECD 1999, 10).

E-commerce accounts for the fastest growing form of commerce in the 21st century and was estimated to continue to grow at double digit rates from 2016 to 2021 (Laudon and Traver 2017, 7). According to Laudon and Traver (2017), e-commerce has led to a number of benefits such as the opening of digital markets, increased transparency (e.g. prices), ease of access, and more efficient cross-border trade. The OECD defines the e-commerce impact as follows: "[T]he internet has done for electronic commerce what Henry Ford did for the automobile—converted a luxury for the few into a relatively simple and inexpensive device for the many" (1999, 10). The presence of e-commerce had already started contributing to important changes in the way B2B and B2C transactions, particularly in the communications, finance, and retail trade industries, take place, as well as consumer behavior, as described in a 1999 OECD report. The same report predicted that e-commerce

> holds promise in areas such as education, health, and government (about 20 per cent of GDP) ... As both a product and manifestation of such transformations, electronic commerce is being shaped by, and increasingly will help to shape, modern society as a whole especially in the areas of education, health, and government services.
>
> **(OECD 1999, 9, 16)**

E-commerce began as an electronic avenue mostly for online retail sales (Laudon and Traver 2017, 7). Over a decade later, the continuous growth, changes, and significance when it comes to commerce and consumer behavior continue to ring true, including in the areas predicted by the same 1999 OECD report.

As consumers expect expediency and efficiency, as well as a positive customer service experience, many companies have to address the challenge of meeting those needs in order to become more competitive in the digital economy. The other benefit of e-commerce is that it decentralizes the playing field so that companies of all sizes, not just the large firms, can sell a product through e-commerce platforms and/or just reach consumers for both goods and services globally with far less time and money. Smaller firms may in fact benefit from the opportunities offered by electronic commerce as they are unencumbered by existing relationships with traditional retail outlets or a large sales force. They may adopt a business model that forces larger, established competitors to restructure their existing relationships or be seen as noncompetitive. The Internet can level the competitive playing field by allowing small companies to extend their geographical reach and secure new customers in ways formerly restricted to much larger firms (OECD 1999, 16, 24).

The key thing to keep in mind is the ability for a business to use technology to market a service to consumers via blogs, quick reply to questions, and search engine optimization. A number of apps have been developed to allow companies to enhance their visibility and interaction with potential clients beyond the immediate commercial transaction, in which payment or money is exchanged for a specific service. Some of these apps, enabled through digital technology, include video conference software and those that allow for real-time responses on a webpage; video streaming services, such as YouTube; and social media platforms that allow for more personal connections with followers through live video options.

"Today, e-commerce has become the platform for media and new, unique services and capabilities that aren't found in the physical world. … The internet is about to replace television as the largest entertainment platform. Welcome to the new e-commerce!" (Laudon and Traver 2017, 7). For example, Facebook, Twitter, Google, Pinterest, iTunes, and Tumblr have grown in importance for media purposes, but Facebook also has a feature that allows for sending and receiving money, and purchasing online. These authors focus on the linkages between e-commerce and entertainment, but this chapter still focuses on e-commerce from a commercial transactional perspective.

The infrastructure of e-commerce has also resulted in the boom of mobile platforms such as iphones and ipads, and tablet computers have been used to conduct commercial transactions. Over a decade later, the growth of these platforms continues and alters the way in which business is conducted and consumer behavior. Also, the rise of e-commerce and the digital technologies discussed later in the chapter have another important role across the board in terms of access to resources, such as financing.

Blockchain Technology

Blockchain technology received much attention when a whitepaper on Bitcoin was released by Satoshi Nakamoto in 2008 and the technology was put to use a year later. Bitcoin is a cryptocurrency* driven by blockchain technology. However, blockchain's origins go as far back as the 1990s when Stuart Haber and W. Scott Stornetta developed secure chain blocks through cryptography that prevented anyone tampering with document timestamps. Their findings appeared in their 1991 paper titled, "How to Time-Stamp a Digital Document." Blockchain has continued to evolve into uses beyond cryptocurrency. It is, first, important to include a reminder as to what blockchain is.

> Simply put, blockchain is a shared ledger, used to record transactions, track assets, improve visibility, and build trust in supply chain networks around the world. Immutable records mean no participant in a network can change information once it has been recorded, meaning errors must be reversed instead of covered up.
>
> **(Grimshaw 2020)**

The key benefit of blockchain technology today is the existence of smart contracts, in which "rules are stored on the chain and automatically executed, meaning conditions for corporate bond transfers, terms for travel insurance to be paid and much more can be defined quickly, and with great ease" (Grimshaw 2020).

As Hughes et al. (2019, 278) explain, cryptocurrency and smart contracts are a part of the first and second phases of blockchain technology. The third phase is blockchain technology's broader societal use. In the latter phase, blockchain technology can lead to greater efficiency and innovation in supply chains and industries such as the healthcare industry (Hughes et al. 2019). Although digital currency remained the leading use of blockchain technology in 2020 at 33%, other uses followed such as data access/sharing, 32%; data reconciliation, 31%; identity protection, 31%; and payments, 30% (Deloitte 2020).

Briefly on Artificial Intelligence

These are other technologies that are not discussed at length here, since the main focus of the chapter is on the digital technologies that allow for

---

* Countries may use a different term when referring to cryptocurrency. For instance digital currency is used in Argentina, Thailand, and Australia; virtual commodity in Canada, China, and Taiwan; crypto-token in Germany; payment token in Switzerland; cyber currency in Italy and Lebanon; electronic currency in Colombia and Lebanon; and virtual asset in Honduras and Mexico ("Regulation of Cryptocurrency Around the World," 2018, p. 1).

increased access to other markets. However, in some discussions with an emphasis on technology, AI is mentioned. Artificial intelligence improves the processes and operations through automation, which allows for the enhancement of products and services.

There are varying definitions as to exactly what is meant by Artificial Intelligence. AI is the "broader concept of machines being able to carry out tasks in a way that we could consider 'smart'" (Marr 2016). Although a broad concept, this type of AI has narrow applied functions, also referred to as weak AI, in which it can carry out specific tasks such as driving a car, completing translation services, and filling out a form (Marr 2016; Jain 2018; Meltzer 2018). The general application, or strong AI, which is still being researched and developed, refers to "self-learning systems that can learn from experience with humanlike breadth and surpass human performance on all tasks" (Meltzer 2018).

According to Davenport (2019), 25–30% of large companies are already going after AI in an aggressive form and have access to the data to do so. On the other hand, smaller firms, as well as B2B firms and basic manufacturing companies, use AI at a far lower rate, because they do not have substantial access to data and also do not possess the proper expertise and awareness (Davenport 2019). The United States, China, the United Kingdom, Canada, and Singapore are some of the countries that are pursuing AI at a fast pace. The way in which AI helps to improve operational processes so that they are more efficient is that tasks can now be automated (Brynjolfsson and McAfee 2019). (For a detailed overview of AI versus machine learning, as well as the categories within AI, see Marr 2016.)

Services Exports in a Digital Economy

The term *digital economy* has been used throughout. What does this term mean? Using the definition by Deloitte:

> It's the economic activity that results from billions of everyday online connections among people, businesses, devices, data, and processes. The backbone of the digital economy is hyperconnectivity which means growing interconnectedness of people, organisations, and machines that results from the Internet, mobile technology and the internet of things (IoT).

The three main traditional sectors that drive economies are agriculture, manufacturing, and services. The 21st century has shown the continued growth and greater impact of the digital sector, which refer to "the producers at the core of digitalization: online platforms, platform-enabled services, and suppliers of ICT goods and services" (IMF 2018, 7). Expanding on what is meant by platform-enabled services, an IMF policy paper titled, "Measuring the Digital Economy," says:

> Platform-enabled services include the sharing economy, whose main components are peer-to-peer short-term property rentals and peer-to-peer labor services (e.g., Uber). Collaborative finance (e.g., peer-to-peer lending) may also be included in the sharing economy. Platform-enabled services to businesses in the "gig economy" include crowdsourcing platforms (e.g., Freelancer and Upwork).

> **(2018, 7)**

This section looks at the digital economy, as a whole, in which different services exports have been transformed by the producers in the digital sector. For instance, healthcare and educational exports are supported by platforms such as WhatsApp and Zoom. The section goes a step further to include those industries, such as finance and logistics/transportation, that have been able to provide services via peer-to-peer-based technologies (i.e., blockchain technology).

Healthcare. During the global health crisis in 2020, ways of providing continued healthcare services domestically and internationally became very important. The boost in healthcare services, such as through the widespread dissemination of information quickly; meeting with patients virtually in response to the stay-at-home or shelter-in-place orders and lockdowns and individuals who had to quarantine; and, in some countries, sending medical doctors from one country to another. In the cases that relied on the use of technology to reach worldwide without the physical movement of people was through digital technology.

Prior to the health pandemic caused by the coronavirus, digital technology has been slow to adoption, even in the face of glaring inefficiencies. For instance, within the industry itself, there have been challenges associated with inefficiencies in the exchange of information between health record vendors, providers, insurance companies, research organizations, and patients (Hughes et al. 2019, 278). Consequently, there have been data breaches and slow access to patient data leading to slower treatment, for which blockchain technology could prove revolutionary in changing the way that health information is stored and exchanged (Hughes et al. 2019, 278). Blockchain is just one form of digital technology that is being studied in an effort to address some of the aforementioned challenges in the healthcare industry. Digital technology, as a part of the Fourth Industrial Revolution (aka Industry 4.0), has also been studied in terms of reducing the costs associated with healthcare as life expectancy increases and the population continues to grow older and the rate of adoption of such technologies both in emerging and developed economies (Tortorella, et al 2020).

The World Health Organization (WHO) even touted the significant role that digital technology, in general, has played in the international healthcare system.

> Digital technologies of all kinds have become essential resources in primary care and their uptake is growing, with the past decade seeing rapid integration of technology in a range of areas that support primary care and essential public health functions. In this context, common uses of digital technologies include searching medical knowledge resources, facilitating clinical support, monitoring quality of care, and mapping and monitoring the spread of infectious diseases, as well as tracking supplies of drugs and vaccines.
>
> **(WHO 2020, 2)**

Even with such progress, the COVID-19 health pandemic exposed the limitations of the healthcare system in many countries, including the United States. "It seems clear that we need an immediate digital revolution to face this crisis," according to Keesara et al. (2020). The rapid pace at which the coronavirus spread globally in a matter of weeks highlighted a healthcare system unable to keep up, because of the limited use of digital technologies due to high regulations in the United States and emphasis on predominantly in-person care.

However, with digital technology, other types of healthcare services could be exported at a much faster pace. For instance, in response to the COVID-19 pandemic, the WHO used the digital communication platform WhatsApp to share information in different languages (Jackson 2020). Additionally, Apple and Google announced that they would collaborate to develop an app-based contact tracing system. Such a system would entail access to smartphones globally to track new infections and alert the user to the need to self-isolate or offer the option of getting a diagnosis. These examples highlight the opportunities, as well as the challenges that must be considered and addressed, in the export of healthcare services.

As with any new opportunity comes additional risks such as cybersecurity threats and attacks on user privacy. The WHO's effort to spread information about COVID-19 rapidly was thwarted by hackers sending false or inaccurate information and cyber-scammers pretending to represent the WHO to gain access to users' personal information. The end-to-end encryption, a method to prevent third parties other than the sender and the recipient from reading and altering data, makes it harder to identify the origin of the message. The sender of the message encrypts the data. In response to the cyber scammers, the WHO posted a notice stating, "Hackers and cyber scammers are taking advantage of the coronavirus disease (COVID-19) pandemic by sending fraudulent email and WhatsApp messages that attempt to trick you into clicking on malicious links or opening attachments."

Privacy concerns have also emerged regarding the app-based contact tracing proposal. An April 2020 opinion piece that appeared in the *Washington Post* newspaper highlighted the threat to privacy with the app-based tracing proposal (Shevlane et al. 2020). A month later the *Washington Post* editorial board printed an editorial expressing concern that the technology could also lead to an attack on the basic rights to privacy (Editorial Board 2020). Considering that the healthcare industry, as in the case of the United States, may have regulations to ensure patient and consumer privacy, any healthcare- or medical-related services export, particularly those delivered through digital technology, will have to also take into account the need to ensure privacy and reduce cyberthreats.

Financial. Chapter 2 highlighted the importance of financial and insurance services exports globally from a historical perspective. It mentioned the role of technology in changing the way in which these services are traded globally. Now, the financial services are a part of the Fourth Industrial Revolution, in which the financial technology (fintech) industry has emerged. Digital technology has revolutionized the export of financial services, which is among the top services exports globally. This offers a detailed insight into how financial service providers use digital technology to reach consumers in overseas markets.

Financial services are provided online digitally in various areas including payment, lending, and insurance. Distributed ledger technology is used in all three services. However, payment services only used distributed technology, which has shifted from physical to virtual form, whereas lending and insurance services also rely on other technologies, such as Internet of Things (IoT) and Artificial Intelligence (AI). Other technologies are limited in terms of their application to the various types of financial services offered (OECD 2018, 14). Digital payments can take place online or via mobile networks and incorporate "online banking, electronic commerce (e.g. Amazon), and payment services (e.g. PayPal)" (OECD 2018, 15).

The digital peer-to-peer payment model has been used for cross-border payments. Cryptocurrency, such as Bitcoin and Ether, are used and stored via digital wallets on a smartphone. There are several sites on how to accept this type of payment for business owners.

While cryptocurrency continues to grow, it is important to understand the regulatory environment governing the use of these types of payments at the national level of the country of interest, if national-level regulation pertaining to cryptocurrency does exist. Because of the volatility and lack of regulation of cryptocurrency, some national-level governments have taken measures to regulate the cryptocurrency. For instance, a 2018 survey by the Law Library of Congress revealed that countries, such as Australia and Canada, have regulated cryptocurrency under laws pertaining to money-laundering and counter-terrorism financing ("Regulation of Cryptocurrency Around the World" 2018, 1). Other countries have restricted transactions and activities involving cryptocurrency at the local level while permitting the use of cryptocurrency beyond the domestic border, as in the cases of Qatar and Bahrain. Cryptocurrency activities and transactions are banned altogether in other countries, specifically in Algeria, Bolivia, Morocco, Nepal, Pakistan, and Vietnam ("Regulation of Cryptocurrency Around the World" 2018, p. 2). Finally, some economies have developed their own cryptocurrency, as in the cases of Venezuela, the East Caribbean Central Bank (ECCB) member states, Lithuania, and the Marshall Islands ("Regulation of Cryptocurrency Around the World" 2018, 2).

Digital technology may allow a company to reach consumers that have long been left out of the traditional credit and banking system. To use digital technology to accept cross-border payments directly, a company can register with an exchange with a digital wallet for accepting payments such as Bitstamp, Coinbase, Coinmama, and Kraken (Azzara 2020).

Logistics and Supply Chain Management. Digital technology and supply chain management are interconnected and interrelated. Global managers can use blockchain, and industry leaders can use technology to improve the processes associated with moving goods internationally and thus give those in the logistics industry a competitive advantage globally. Ninety percent of world trade is conducted by the shipping industry each year (DHL 2018, 13). Reducing supply chain barriers to trade could increase global gross domestic product by nearly 5% and global trade by 15% (DHL 2018, 13). The global logistics company, DHL, describes the link between technology and the industry as follows:

> Like a pebble dropped into a lake, the ripples from this technology are beginning to expand outwards in all directions including the logistics industry, where blockchain promises to make business processes more efficient and facilitate innovative new services and business models.
>
> **(2018, 21)**

The industry, much like the discussion regarding healthcare, is plagued with a lot of inefficiencies caused by long processes and players involved—buyer, seller, warehouse operator, transport company, banks, insurance, customs—and the paperwork and documentation. According to a 2018 DHL report, there are more than 500,000 trucking companies in the United States alone, 50,000 merchant ships in the global shipping industry, and numerous customs authorities regulating the passage of freight (p. 13). The same report uses the example of one shipment of refrigerated goods from East Africa to Europe having to deal with 30 people and organizations with over 200 different types of interactions, thereby illustrating a very time-consuming and costly process (p. 13). Because so many stakeholders are involved in the supply chain process, the result is the lack of transparency, a harmonized process, decentralized access to information, and varying levels of technological advances. The company proposes that blockchain can create a more efficient, transparent, traceable, and error-free system (DHL 2018, 12).

Education/Training. Throughout most of the 21st century business leaders, educational organizations, and government agencies had started using digital technologies, especially e-commerce, to reach wider audiences, generate leads, and sell a service for a fee.

The 2020 health pandemic forced many more businesses and organizations to embrace technology fully to stay relevant, visible, and operational throughout the economic uncertainty and slowdown. Sitting in virtual business networking sessions has raised the questions as to how companies are pivoting, a common theme that has emerged has been the greater dependence on technology to meet with clients, to share a message, and offer a service. Digital technology has played a role in allowing service providers to offer educational services ranging from digital marketing programs to supply chain management to developing a strategy to compete in other markets.

When it comes to education, many learning management systems, such as Blackboard and Canvas, were enhanced with the use of video conferencing platforms, such as Zoom, Cisco Webex, Microsoft Teams, and Adobe Connect, to allow for interactive and engaging virtual classrooms.

The technologies available are just tools to allow service providers to connect without the traditional method and costs associated with traveling overseas and meeting face-to-face to gain exposure for a service and/or to provide the service itself. To leverage these technologies to reach a global market, the traditional need for developing a strategy for competing in those markets remains. The case studies below offer insight into two companies. The first company shed light on the things that a service provider must take into consideration when using e-commerce. The second case is based on a digital marketing firm and how it has been able to reach consumers in the United States and Ghana, as well as throughout Europe and other parts of the African continent.

The digital sector impacts other areas of everyday life worldwide that is definitely worth mentioning. For instance, Google is a worldwide platform for conducting internet searches, storing information, and document sharing. Facebook is another online platform. WhatsApp was already mentioned earlier. The ride-sharing services, Uber and Lyft, have a global presence. Airbnb, which offers lodging services, has a presence around the globe. All of these rely on digital technology, rather than traditional methods, to provide these services all around the world. Other specific platforms exist focused on cross-border communication with specific countries, such as WeChat, which allows for cross-border telecommunication with the Chinese market. While these examples are often cited, the two case studies that follow look at how two small companies are having a greater impact on other companies—small, medium, and large.

CASE STUDY 8.1 USING E-COMMERCE TO HELP FIRMS WITH INTERNATIONAL SALES

"There is a science to it, but at the end of the day, it's the art of selling online."

Hema Dey, Owner, President, CEO, Iffel International

When talking about reaching global markets via e-commerce, Iffel International offers a scientific approach to helping its clients' business gain greater visibility on search engines, such as Google, usually through its search engine optimization (SEO), *inter alia*, services. The ultimate goal is to translate that visibility into sales for a firm. At the same time, the firm's owner, Hema Dey, stresses that there is also an art to making a sale online, which is shared as a general guide for companies looking to make sales in a foreign market in today's business climate.

E-commerce refers to the buying and selling of goods and services through electronic means, whether through a shopping cart on a website or generating leads for the services provided, according to Ms. Dey. Furthermore, Ms. Dey defines digital marketing as follows:

> Digital marketing … encompasses strategy, branding, messaging, SEO, which involves designs and development of websites; and then the formulation of what needs to happen to get particular key words and key phrases ranked on the first page of Google. To do that, we do blogging, social media, e-mail marketing, advertising, whatever it takes to fuel traffic to the website and then with the ultimate goal of sales, which is why I branded [Iffel International] SEO2Sales.

One thing to understand when trying to make that sale is the psychology of the buyer. More specifically, asking questions such as: *What does the buyer want? What are my competitors doing to reach the buyers? What can my firm do differently?* "So to really get a good e-commerce platform put together, it's not just about what you have but understanding buyer psychology," Ms. Dey adds. Having a grasp on the buyer psychology and your competitors becomes even more important in today's times when more people are spending quite a bit of time online due to the COVID-19 pandemic.

There are tangible things that can be done to tap into that buyer psychology. Developing a website that speaks to the emotion of the buyer should lead to increased engagement and, eventually, sales.

The other key piece of the puzzle is having the site ranked at the top of a search engine, such as Google, by being visible and presenting a solution to a specific problem. "[T]here is now an artificial intelligence that can track information based on a search so that your site or your information can be presented in a form of remarketing," says Ms. Dey.

So how has this method worked for other companies? Iffel International mainly works with other service providers, such as doctors and attorneys, as well as manufacturers of engineering-based products. In one case with a medium-sized* third-party-logistics (3PL) company that delivers goods to businesses such as Walmart and Target, "what I did with them was with their website is recreate content to present them as a West Coast (USA) solution for East Coast companies but also international companies coming in through the Port of Los Angeles." As a result, the logistics firm has generated leads from international companies and has reached a point where it needed to move to a new facility located in Fullerton, California.

The key international markets with which Iffel International works and offers international leads for U.S. companies are Europe, Asia, Australia, and New Zealand, including for the 3PL company, which, according to Ms. Dey, has seen significant growth over the last eight to nine years.

Even in Iffel International's case, it has provided cross-border services to an international company looking to export to the United States in the past. Working with a high-end New Zealand sheepskin rug manufacturing company, Ms. Dey's approach helped to increase the company's presence in the U.S. market through more targeted lead generation, which, in turn, led to finding new customers and getting the sales. However, as Ms. Dey explained, currently all of Iffel International's clients are U.S. companies that receive support with reaching and making sales in the overseas market.

What are the challenges that firms face? Many companies appear to still face the hurdle of just understanding the value of digital marketing and developing an appropriate strategy. According to Ms. Dey:

> So pre-Covid, it was very much two camps, one that bought into it and understood the value of it, but then there were others who … didn't want to pay for it. So they didn't see value in it. But, post Covid, we saw the whole world shut down … It pretty much went from e-nothing to e-everything.
>
> Now, the acceleration of everything has been so impactful that when lockdown happened I saw three camps of entrepreneurs and

---

* Although the term *medium sized* was used to describe the size of the company being discussed by the interviewee, the interview did not lead to defining exactly what is meant by medium sized when it comes to number of employees or annual revenue. Nevertheless, medium- or mid-sized companies have been defined as a revenue of US$10 million to US$1 billion and, in international terms, between 50 and 250 employees (Merritt 2019).

business owners: the ones that are conservative, they saw a lock-down that could spin the whole economy into a recession and they cut their digital marketing budget. And you have the ones that had an intense budget and cut it back down, because they didn't know what to do …. And the ones that went and pumped in and invested in this down time and realized if you are not visible, you are nobody.

And so what happened was that companies that were paying and were ranked got deranked, because they were not investing any-more; and the ones that invested, who were not ranked, came up!

The lesson is that using digital marketing, including SEO strategy, to increase the visibility of the service that one provides is very important. However, there must be a well-developed approach that allows a business to tap into the emo-tions and the psychology of the end-user, including in the overseas market.

Google is going to be a really important good source for compet-ing for your business. Social media is super critical, too, because everyone is on their cellphones … You need to use it wisely and adapt and apply the methodology to social media to what you are trying to sell to connect to the buyer.

CASE STUDY 8.2 A DIGITAL MARKETING FIRM CONNECTS AFRICA, NORTH AMERICA, AND EUROPE

Don't come in with a Western strategy. Think about a solution that works for the demographics that you are trying to cultivate.

Mac Maison, co-founder, Atunwa Digital

Atunwa Digital was founded in 2018. The company provides services to other companies in countries around the world such as the United States, Germany, and Kenya, just to name a few. Atunwa Digital's co-founder, Mac Maison, who has been in the digital media industry for six years and is based in the West African country of Ghana, explains that:

Atunwa Digital provides digital media solutions for companies that are into advertising and the media groups that put audio content,

> video content, and written content over their websites and mobile apps. We connect advertisers with these content pieces ... and for media groups, we also provide them with extensive training on ad operations, because oftentimes in Africa, there's a deficit of skilled labor when it comes to digital media. So we like to be able to provide training and information sharing to our clients, as well.

In addition, Atunwa Digital offers its services to those U.S. and European firms looking to reach African diaspora groups or the citizens of specific countries throughout the African region. In the United States specifically, Atunwa Digital has delivered campaigns for large, well-known retail companies.

Atunwa Digital implements both a direct and indirect strategy to reach clients in countries worldwide looking to advertise their brands to consumers on the African continent, as Mr. Maison shares further.

> So we have partnerships with certain companies in the U.S. that put us in touch with agencies. In addition to that, we also do our own direct campaigns to agencies where we connect with them, share with them our information about the type of inventories we have, and then help them with the sales process. It's a combination of having partners to connect us with agencies and us going directly to them.

When discussing some of the advertiser markets that have contributed to Atunwa's revenue growth, Mr. Maison provided the following estimates:

- United States—20%
- United Kingdom—30%
- Germany—20%
- Italy—20%
- Ghana—5%

The remaining five percent is spread across other markets. Some of the other markets mentioned that receive Atunwa Digital's services include Kenya, Nigeria, France, the Netherlands, and Spain.

Unforeseen challenges affecting the global economy and community can have a serious impact on a global company's growth and competitive strategy, as in the case of the COVID-19 crisis. Atunwa Digital has experienced challenges in 2020, as a result. More specifically, advertising experienced a decline and budgets were cut.

However, the company has also developed ways to address the needs of clients during such a time of uncertainty. According to Mr. Maison:

> More companies have been interested in how they can create additional value for their digital inventories. Digital has been on the backburner for a lot of African creators, and that's partially the challenge of associating with producing the content, keeping the content online, and getting the user access without piracy.

> So, because they weren't able to figure out solutions for all those things, they kind of just let it go where they had a "content every-where strategy" to build a large audience. But as the pandemic set in and they realized that a lot of their revenues were being cut, they wanted to determine what strategy they needed to put in place to capitalize off of their digital inventories. That has created a lot more conversations for us where we were able to use our track record with our existing clients. A lot of times our clients brought other clients to us. It's been helpful where we have this track record to be able to showcase to potential clients that this is what we've done, this is what we can do for you, and this is what the future of digital holds.

Some of these conversations have turned into a client-base for Atunwa Digital in the midst of the pandemic.

Several factors have contributed to Atunwa Digital's success reaching markets around the globe. Mr. Maison credits the network that he has developed internationally, especially from his work in the area of international development for over a decade. Building such relationships, including those with clients, has opened up opportunities for the firm.

When developing a strategy for doing business in an overseas market, such as Ghana, it is important to understand that country's way of doing business. Mr. Maison says:

> One of the challenges that I've seen a lot of people do … is they have this Western approach, and that doesn't work out here. When it comes down to doing business and getting things done, you have to throw all of that out of the window and kind of understand

exactly what the clients' needs are [and] what the client is comfortable with doing in terms of the process of getting business done, and from there form your strategy.

Bibliography

Aljifri, Hassan A.; Alexander Pons; and Daniel Collins. 2003. "Global e-commerce: a framework for understanding and overcoming the trust barrier." *Information Management and Computer Security* 11 (3):130–138.

Azzara, Mike. 2020. "Breaking the crypto code: How to accept cryptocurrency payments." *American Express*. Accessed August 24, 2020. https://www.ame ricanexpress.com/us/foreign-exchange/articles/how-to-accept-cryptocurrency-payments-for-smes/.

Brynjolfsson, Erik; and McAfee Andrew. 2019. "The business of artificial intelligence." In *Artificial Intelligence: The Insights You Need from Harvard Business Review (HBR insights series)*, edited by Thomas H. Davenport; Erik Brynjolfsson; Andrew McAfee, and H. James Wilson. Boston: Harvard Business Review Press, 12–20.

Columbus, Louis. 2020. "How Covid-19 is Transforming E-Commerce." *Forbes*. Accessed September 30, 2020. https://www.forbes.com/sites/louiscolumbus/2020/04/28/how-covid-19-is-transforming-e-commerce/?sh=70c7e92b3544.

Davenport, Thomas H. 2019. "The state of AI in business." In *Artificial intelligence: The Insights You Need from Harvard Business Review (HBR insights series)*, edited by Erik Brynjolfsson, Andrew Mcafee and James H. Wilson. Boston: Harvard Business Review Press.

Deloitte. 2020. "Blockchain technology use cases in organizations worldwide as of 2020*." Chart. June 16, 2020. Statista. Accessed August 29, 2020. https://www.statista.com/statistics/878732/worldwide-use-cases-blockchain-technology/.

Deloitte. n.d. "What is digital economy?" Accessed August 31, 2020. https://www2.deloitte.com/mt/en/pages/technology/articles/mt-what-is-digital-economy.html.

Dalsey, Hillblom, and Lynn (DHL). 2018. *Blockchain in Logistics*. Troisdorf, Germany: DHL Customer Solutions & Innovation.

Editorial Board. 2020. "Before we use digital contact tracing, we must weigh the costs." *Washington Post*. Accessed September 6, 2020. https://www.washingtonpost.com/opinions/tech-firms-must-prove-that-digital-contact-tracing-is-worth-the-privacy-intrusion/2020/05/01/cbf19b8e-7dc7-11ea-9040-68981f488eed_story.html.

Grimshaw, Jack. 2020. "IBM Blockchain: What is Blockchain Technology?" *Supply Chain Digital Magazine*. Accessed September 30, 2020. https://www.supplychaindigital.com/technology/ibm-blockchain-what-blockchain-technology.

Haber, Stuart; and W. Scott Stornetta. 1991. "How to time-stamp a digital document." *Journal of Cryptology* 3 (2):99–111.

Hughes, Alex; Andrew Park; Jan Kietzmann; and Chris Archer-Brown. 2019. "Beyond Bitcoin: What blockchain and distributed ledger technologies mean for firms." In *Business Horizons* 62:273–281.

IMF (International Monetary Fund). 2018. *Measuring the Digital Economy.* Washington, DC: International Monetary Fund.

Jackson, Sarita. 2020. "Increased digitalisation of services trade in today's global economic paralysis." *World Financial Review*, June 10, https://worldfinanci alreview.com/increased-digitalisation-of-services-trade-in-todays-global-ec onomic-paralysis/.

Jain, Anjli. 2018. "What's narrow Al and how it's paving the way for the future." *Entrepreneur.com.* https://www.entrepreneur.com/article/310261.

Keesara, M. D., Sirina; Andrea Jonas, M. D.; and Kevin Schulman, M. D. 2020. "COVID-19 and health care's digital revolution." *New England Journal of Medicine.* 382: e82.

Koetsier, John. 2020. "Covid-19 Accelerated E-Commerce Growth 4 to 6 years." *Forbes.* Accessed September 30, 2020. https://www.forbes.com/sites/johnkoetsier/2020 /06/12/covid-19-accelerated-e-commerce-growth-4-to-6-years/#55611407600f.

Laudon, Kenneth C.; and Carol Guercio Traver. 2017. *E-Commerce: Business, Technology and Society.* London: Pearson.

Marr, Bernard. 2016. "What is the Difference Between Artificial Intelligence and Machine Learning?" *Forbes.* Accessed September 30, 2020. https://www.forbes .com/sites/bernardmarr/2016/12/06/what-is-the-difference-between-artificial-i ntelligence-and-machine-learning/?sh=70a0b67e2742.

Meltzer, Joshua P. 2018. "The impact of artificial intelligence on international trade." In *A Blueprint for the Future of AI.* Washington, DC: Brookings.

Merritt, Cam. 2019. "What size company is considered a mid-size company?" March 8. *Small Business Chronicle.* Accessed August 24, 2020. https://smallbusiness .chron.com/size-company-considered-midsize-company-71776.html.

Organization for Economic Cooperation (OECD). 1999. "Economic and Social Impact of Electronic Impact of E-commerce." In *Preliminary Finds and Research Agenda OECD Digital Economy Papers*, 3–166. Paris, France: OECD.

OECD. 2018. *Financial Markets, Insurance and Private Pensions: Digitalisation and Finance.* Paris, France: OECD.

"Regulation of cryptocurrency around the world." 2018. *Library of Congress.* Accessed August 24, 2020. https://www.loc.gov/law/help/cryptocurrency/c ryptocurrency-world-survey.pdf.

Shevlane, Toby; Ben Garfinkeland; and Allan Dafoe. 2020. "Contact tracing apps can help stop coronavirus. But they can hurt privacy." *Washington Post.* Accessed September 6, 2020. https://www.washingtonpost.com/politics/2020/ 04/28/contact-tracing-apps-can-help-stop-coronavirus-they-can-hurt-privacy/.

Tortorella, Guilherme Luz et al. 2020. "Effects of contingencies on healthcare 4.0 technologies adoption and barriers in emerging economies." *Technological Forecasting and Social Change* 156: 1–11.

WHO (World Health Organization). "Digital technologies: Shaping the future of primary health care." *World Health Organization.* Accessed September 6, 2020. https://apps.who.int/iris/handle/10665/326573.

POLICIES AND INSTITUTIONS GOVERNING TRADE IN SERVICES

Chapter 9

Evolution of the Multilateral Framework for Trade in Services

By the late 1980s, it became apparent that governments around the world understood the significance of services as a tradable commodity in the global economy. More specifically, in September 1986, trade negotiators representing the contracting parties to the General Agreement on Tariffs and Trade (GATT) met in Punta del Este, Uruguay to reform the international trade system. (Contracting parties refer to the countries and territories that are members of GATT.) For the next 7.5 years, during what is known as the Uruguay Round of negotiations, the contracting parties engaged in talks that produced a multilateral framework that now includes measures governing trade in services and established the World Trade Organization (WTO). The additional measures to address a more complex global economy applied to all GATT contracting parties, which are now referred to as WTO members.

The international-level institutions governing international trade in services and goods are set by national-level governments. In other words, national-level representatives for each member economy can shape the international-level policies. It is these policies that shape, not just the trade policies of the domestic governments, but rather the trade practices of sectors, industries, and firms. Furthermore, these international and multilateral policies may help or hinder the ability for a sector, industry, and firm's ability to compete both at home and internationally.

Because of the impact of domestic government players on international trade policies that impact businesses, this chapter, along with the following two chapters, discusses the often overlooked and misunderstood institutions. To fully understand the existing trade system, it is first necessary to briefly underscore the historical evolution of the international trade framework.

A multilateral trade system emerged as a response to World War II. International leaders recognized the need for a multilateral economic system as a means to achieving long-lasting peace and security. On August 14, 1941, U.S. President Franklin D. Roosevelt and UK Prime Minister Winston Churchill met aboard the USS Augusta (CA-31) in Placentia Bay, Newfoundland to produce what became known as the Atlantic Charter. The Atlantic Charter consisted of a total of eight principle clauses outlining the U.S. and British goals for the world following the end of World War II. Clause 4 focused on lowering trade barriers, and Clause 5 promoted economic cooperation globally. "The Charter was not only the genesis of several remarkable achievements of multilateral international economic rule-making, including the General Agreement on Tariffs and Trade and Bretton Woods institutions, but also paved the way for an unprecedented era of relative peace and security," writes Nottage (2020) in a WTO article.

On October 30, 1947, six years after the Atlantic Charter, 23 countries and territories signed GATT. The contracting parties included Australia, Belgium, Brazil, Burma (present-day Myanmar), Canada, Ceylon (present-day Sri Lanka), Chile, China, Cuba, Czechoslovakia (present-day Czech Republic and Slovakia), France, India, Lebanon, Luxembourg, Netherlands, New Zealand, Norway, Pakistan, Southern Rhodesia (present-day Zimbabwe), Syria, South Africa, United Kingdom, and the United States. Six of the founding parties— Belgium, Canada, Luxembourg, the Netherlands, the United Kingdom, and the United States—also committed to provisionally apply the GATT and its tariff concession on or after January 1, 1948. "What is perhaps less known is that GATT, as an international treaty, never entered into force either," writes Counsellor of the Market Access Division of the WTO Roy Santana (2017, 20). Santana is referring to the similarity between GATT's outcome and that of the formal organization, International Trade Organization (ITO), which did not take effect. The Counsellor goes further to write,

> Unknown to the 23 delegations ... it was the signing of the PPA [Protocol of Provisional Application] by those six "key" countries, and not the 23 signatures of the "Final Act" of the GATT which ultimately provided the legal hook that saved the multilateral trading system.

(Santana 2017, p. 20)

The reason being varying interests led to discord and disagreements that almost threatened the realization of GATT.

The creation of an official organization to enforce trade rules also faltered. Separate negotiations took place with the intent to establish the ITO. These talks occurred during the Bretton Woods Conference (July 1–22, 1944). The original intent behind the ITO was to establish an agency within the United Nations that would promote an increase in trade flows worldwide through the elimination or reduction of tariffs, as well as other barriers to trade. The plans to create an ITO remained dormant, but the Bretton Woods Conference produced two other important organizations— the International Monetary Fund (IMF) and the International Bank for Reconstruction and Development (IBRD), which is the lending branch of the World Bank.

ITO negotiations were scheduled for completion in 1948 in Havana, Cuba. Due to opposition in the U.S. Congress, U.S. President Harry Truman withdrew U.S. support, which, eventually, resulted in the failure of the ITO to come to fruition. Nevertheless, the Final Act of the United Nations Conference on Trade and Employment (also known as the Final Act of the Havana Charter) was successfully signed by 53 governments on March 24, 1948 (see also UNCTAD). Nevertheless, international trade rules for goods were set and enforced under GATT from 1948 to 1994.

Since GATT took effect, the international trade system became more complex. As the number of contracting parties to GATT grew, the differences in economic development had to be taken into account. Also, there was a need to address additional traded sectors. Furthermore, international trade faced additional challenges, such as increased regulatory barriers to trade and concerns about intellectual property rights in foreign markets.

One additional traded sector that caught the attention of some of the GATT contracting parties was the services sector. The services sector gained prominence because its trade flows continued to increase at a faster pace. The services sector trade flows grew to the point of surpassing that of trade in goods. More specifically, trade in services globally jumped from 17% to 20% of global trade from 1980 to 1990 (Hoekman and Braga 1997). The rapid growth in services trade can be attributed to the following factors:

■ The rise of internet communication and digital technologies;
■ The growing interconnectedness between goods and services;
■ The services sector employment outpacing that of manufacturing in many of the OECD countries; and

▪ The movement toward services specialization in an effort to increase productivity (Marchetti and Mavroidis 2011, 691).

The ever-growing services trade was met with protectionism in the services sector. The measures used to restrict cross-border trade in services have included outright restrictions; quantitative restrictions in the form of quotas, price controls set by the government; local content requirements; and discriminatory market access practices (Hoekman and Braga 1997). Air service agreements may limit the number of airlines that can fly via a particular route, which is an example of a quantitative restriction on services trade (see Hoekman and Braga 1997 for more).

The liberalization of trade in services was addressed during the Uruguay Round of multilateral trade negotiations, which lasted from September 1986 in Punta del Este, Uruguay, to April 1994 in Marrakesh, Morocco. The varying levels of economic development among the negotiators led to different interests and disagreements surrounding the services sector. Developed countries felt that trade liberalization brought about benefits both nationally and internationally. Many of the developing countries, on the other hand, initially opposed including services in the Uruguay Round of negotiations. For example, Indian economists T. N. Sarinivasan and Suresh D. Tendulkar explain, "Brazil and India led a group of developing countries that were strongly opposed on the ground that they were not ready to negotiate on services on an equal footing with industrialized countries" (2003, 80). Because the developing countries lacked the proper resources to negotiate, they were not able to prevent the inclusion of services in the negotiations. "In addition, because of their scarce negotiating resources, they would find it difficult simultaneously to follow negotiations on the traditional GATT agenda (which comprised farm and textiles goods) and on services," write Counsellor at the Trade in Services Division of the WTO Juan A. Marchetti and law professor Petros C. Mavroidis (2011, 698). They go on further to say:

> Developing countries were facing the following dilemma: either continue to say 'no' to the U.S. requests for negotiating a multilateral framework on trade in services, and retain their freedom to define unilaterally the regulation of their services markets, but at the risk of being sanctioned by the U.S.; or enter into services negotiations in the GATT and try to constrain as much as possible the possibility for the U.S. to act unilaterally. Under the circumstances, it should not come as a surprise that some developing countries chose the latter. Almost every account of the negotiations

in Punta del Este points to the fact that the US, and more precisely its USTR, Clayton Yeutter, was one of the decisive factors in pushing services into the agenda of the Uruguay Round.

(2011, 702)

The lack of interest among many of the developing countries in the negotiations surrounding trade in services stemmed from their minimal competitive advantage in the services sector beyond tourism, which was already liberalized (Marchetti and Mavroidis 2011, 698, 707). As a result of the asymmetry in resources between the developed and developing countries during the negotiations, the latter took a passive stance (Kahler and Odell 1989; Finger 2007; Marchetti and Mavroidis 2011).

The updated version of the GATT agreement was completed in 1994 by 128 signatories (hereafter referred to as WTO members). What resulted from the Uruguay Round was the "biggest reform of international trade since the end of the Second World War" via the creation of the World Trade Organization (WTO), which took effect on January 1, 1995 (WTO "History"). The WTO included rules pertaining to trade in services, intellectual property, and an improved dispute settlement process. The Uruguay Round also focused on the liberalization of sensitive sectors such as agriculture and textiles.

The key set of measures for trade in services that came out of the Uruguay Round was the General Agreement on Trade in Services (GATS). GATS established disciplines for specific services, while also extending preferential treatment to lesser developed countries (LDCs).

The Uruguay Round produced other important rules aligned to a more complex trade system. The Trade Related Aspects of Intellectual Property Rights (referred to as TRIPS) established rules to protect the creation from the mind that is applied toward goods and services supplied in another country or territory. Also, the Trade Policy Review Mechanism was established to monitor the domestic trade policies of the WTO members. This information can be accessed on the WTO website, and trade policies can be searched by country and chronological order of the review since 1995. Additionally, the Uruguay Round improved the dispute settlement system, which had already been created under GATT. The system became one with fixed timetables for the dispute settlement process; clarity regarding each stage in the process, including the appeals process; transparency about the rulings; and rulings that automatically take effect so that a losing member cannot block the ruling.

Seven years after the completion of the Uruguay Round, the WTO members began another round of negotiation to further reform the international trade system known as the Doha Round. This round aimed "to produce the first major overhaul of the system in the 21st century," (WTO "Doha Round"). The Doha Round of negotiations were launched in Doha, Qatar, in November 2001. The overall goal of the Doha Round was to deepen trade liberalization and increase market access, while also strengthening the WTO rules. The Doha Round agenda included talks pertaining to agriculture, non-agricultural market access, dispute settlement, and e-commerce.

Unlike the Uruguay Round, the developing countries, especially the larger emerging economies, such as Brazil and South Africa, played a more active role in the negotiations. The developing countries opposed the proposals to further liberalize agriculture, especially while the United States and Western European countries continued to offer trade distorting cotton subsidies to their local farmers (Smith and Rice 2004; Hanrahan and Schnepf 2007). These subsidies would create an unfair competitive advantage for producers in developed countries while harming the producers in developing countries. As a result of the controversy surrounding agricultural subsidies, the talks stalled by the end of the Hong Kong Ministerial in December 2005. There have been efforts to create a blueprint that would be applied toward a final deal, which still has yet to be concluded.

By this time, 157 WTO member governments participated in the Doha Round. Some progress was made with regard to trade in services. For instance, the first major agreement pertaining to preferential treatment in services for LDCs, which came out of the Special Session of the Council for Trade in Services that took place on September 3, 2003. This means that the WTO members agreed to modalities that included offering preferential market access to LDCs when making commitments, as they align with the GATS Negotiations of Specific Commitments (Article XIX). GATS Article XIX "requires members to establish for each round of services negotiations how they will provide special treatment for LDCS. These are known as 'modalities.'" Furthermore, LDCs enjoy the flexibility to allow market access for fewer services-based industries when making commitments to liberalize their markets and may benefit from technical assistance.

> Members shall take into account the serious difficulty of LDCs in undertaking negotiated specific commitments in view of their special economic situation, and therefore shall exercise restraint in seeking commitments from LDCs. In particular, they shall generally not seek the removal of conditions which LDCs may attach when making access to their markets available to foreign service

suppliers to the extent that those conditions are aimed at achieving the objectives of Article IV of the GATS.

There shall be flexibility for LDCs for opening fewer sectors, liberalizing fewer types of transactions, and progressively extending market access in line with their development situation. LDCs shall not be expected to offer full national treatment, nor are they expected to undertake additional commitments under Article XVIII of the GATS on regulatory issues which may go beyond their institutional, regulatory, and administrative capacities. In response to requests, LDCs may make commitments compatible with their development, trade and financial needs and which are limited in terms of sectors, modes of supply and scope.

(WTO "General Agreement on Trade in Services")

The 2005 Hong Kong Ministerial Conference reiterated the economic plight of LDCs. As a result, the LDCs can decide to not adopt new commitments in trade in services.

We urge all Members to participate actively in these negotiations towards achieving a progressively higher level of liberalization of trade in services, with appropriate flexibility for individual developing countries as provided for in Article XIX of the GATS. Negotiations shall have regard to the size of economies of individual Members, both overall and in individual sectors. We recognize the particular economic situation of LDCs, including the difficulties they face, and acknowledge that they are not expected to undertake new commitments.

(WTO "General Agreement on Trade in Services")

In 2011, six years after the Doha Round stalled, the contracting parties agreed to a waiver that granted preferential treatment to those services and service suppliers from LDC member economies (WT/L847). A WTO member from a developed and developing economy must submit a notification to the Council for Trade in Services, after which preferential treatment related to market access (GATS XVI) can be implemented. Preferential treatment for any other GATS measures has to be approved by the Council for Trade

Table 9.1   Treatment of Services in GATT, Uruguay Round, Doha Round

	General Agreement on Tariffs in Trade (GATT)	*Uruguay Round World Trade Organization (WTO)*	*Doha Round WTO*	*Post-Doha WTO*
Includes services	No	Yes	Yes	Yes
Outcome	n/a	General Agreement on Trade in Services (GATS)	Preferential treatment for LDCs	Preferential treatment offered through waiver

in Services. The services waiver for LDC members would stay in effect for 15 years from the date of adoption. The Bali Ministerial Conference, which took place on December 7, 2013, set the steps to encourage the WTO members from the developed and developing economies to use the LDC services waiver. The Doha Round also sought to address other areas such as agriculture, non-agricultural market access, dispute settlement, and e-commerce, although it still has yet to be concluded (Table 9.1).

Besides the LDC services waiver, not much progress was made in other areas to liberalize trade in services, such as tackling the regulatory barriers to trade.

Due to the lack of progress made on the services talks during the Doha Round, several WTO member governments came together and proposed the Trade in Services Agreement (TiSA). In 2012, five WTO member governments, who labeled themselves as the Really Good Friends of Services to demonstrate their commitment to promoting the interests of the services industry, proposed TiSA. The initial group included the European Union, the United States, Canada, Mexico, and Japan. Talks for a plurilateral agreement, which means that the agreement only extends to countries that choose to participate, began in April 2013 and continued through 2016. The talks included 23 parties (22 countries plus the European Union) or a total of 50 countries (22 countries plus the 28 member states of the European Union), which combined account for over two-thirds of global trade in services. The purpose of these talks was to further liberalize trade in services. TiSA would be separate from the WTO and apply only to the 23 parties. The negotiations have remained at a standstill since 2016. The differing perspectives on the opportunities and challenges for service suppliers and participating economies under TiSA have contributed to the controversy surrounding TiSA, which is discussed in greater detail in Chapter 11.

The multilateral trade regime has evolved since the mid-20th century. The push toward economic cooperation focused on removing tariff barriers to trade in goods. The United States and the United Kingdom believed that economic cooperation would contribute to peace following World War II. By the 21st century, the trade regime advanced to include other areas, one of which was the services sector. Discussions surrounding trade in services keeps efforts to address the changes within the services sector, such as the effect of different technologies on the delivery of various types of services, at the forefront. These international-level institutions shape the global business environment within which businesses operate. The outcomes of the negotiations outlined in this chapter affect access to consumers in countries internationally and the ability to compete in one's home market. The next chapter looks at GATS in greater detail, especially the measures that pertain to specific types of services.

Bibliography

Finger, Michael J. 2007. "Implementation and Imbalance: Dealing with hangover from the Uruguay Round." *Oxford Review of Economic Policy* 23 (3): 440–60.

Hanrahan, Charles E.; and Randy Schnepf. 2007. *WTO Doha Round: The Agricultural Negotiations.* Washington, DC: Congressional Research Service.

Hoekman, Bernard; and Carlos A. Primo Braga. 1997. *Protection and Trade in Services.* Washington, D.C.: World Bank.

Kahler, Miles; and John Odell. 1989. "Developing countries coalition: Building and international trade negotiations." In *Developing Countries and the Global Trading System*, edited by John Whalley, 149–167. London: Palgrave Macmillan.

Marchetti, Juan A.; and Petros C. Mavroidis. 2011. "The genesis of the GATS (General Agreement on Trade and Services)" *European Journal of International Law* 22 (3):689–721.

Nottage, Hunter. 2020. "Trade in war's darkest hour: Churchill and Roosevelt's daring Atlantic 1941 meeting that linked global economic cooperation to lasting peace and security." Accessed September 30, 2020. https://www.wto.org/english/thewto_e/history_e/tradewardarkhour41_e.htm.

Santana, Roy. "70th anniversary of the GATT: Stalin, the Marshall Plan, and the provisional application of the GATT 1947." *Journal of Trade Law and Development* 9:1–20.

Sarinivasan, T. N.; and Suresh Tendulkar. 2003. *Reintegrating India with the World Economy.* Washington, DC: Peterson Institute for International Economics.

Smith, Gayle; and Susan Rice. 2004. *WTO Hands a Critical Victory to African Farmers*. Washington, DC: Brookings.

WTO (World Trade Organization). n.d.a. "Doha round: What are they negotiating?" Accessed September 30, 2020. https://www.wto.org/english/tratop_e/dda_e/update_e.htm.

WTO. n.d.b. "General agreement on trade in services." Accessed September 30, 2020. https://www.wto.org/english/tratop_e/serv_e/gatsintr_e.htm.

WTO. n.d.c. "History of the multilateral trading system." Accessed September 30, 2020. https://www.wto.org/english/thewto_e/history_e/history_e.htm#.

Chapter 10

General Agreement on Trade in Services

Jay Cohen, a U.S. citizen, found an opportunity to generate revenue by providing online gambling services from the small Caribbean double-island of Antigua and Barbuda (hereafter referred to as Antigua) to U.S. consumers. Online gambling services are legal in Antigua and require a license. However, U.S. laws were used to argue that online gambling services, in this specific case, were illegal. This business opportunity resulted in Mr. Cohen being arrested in the United States, fined, and sentenced to almost two years in prison. The case against Mr. Cohen eventually became an important landmark dispute settlement case before the WTO and between Antigua and the United States. The international-level dispute case was initiated in 2003 and is known as the United States-Measures Affecting the Cross-border Supply of Gambling and Betting Services case (also referred to as US-Gambling for short). The General Agreement on Trade in Services (GATS) rules were invoked in this dispute case.

GATS took effect on January 1, 1995, and is currently the first and only multilateral agreement covering trade in services. GATS applies to all services and those offered for commercial purposes. There are exceptions to consider. GATS does not cover services provided by the government or those related to the air transport sector. The Council on Trade in Services monitors the implementation of GATS and reports to the General Council.

The agreement creates room for more flexibility in meeting the requirements as a way of addressing the challenges that the developing and the least developed economies faced when satisfying WTO rules.

More specifically, members can decide which services will be a part of the commitment to allow for increased access to foreign suppliers. Furthermore, the members can set limits in the areas of market access and national treatment. Additionally, WTO members do not have to make specific commitments in all modes of supply, as explained in the next section. Rather, they can limit access to the way in which services are provided to any number of the modes of supply. Finally, WTO members can decide to include exemptions to MFN treatment. The flexibility granted to member governments reflects the GATS preamble, which allows for the "right of Members to regulate, and to introduce new regulations, on the supply of services within their territories in order to meet national policy objectives" (WTO "General Agreement on Trade in Services (GATS)"). Each area—market access, national treatment, modes of supply, and most-favoured nation treatment—is explained in the following sections as they pertain to GATS.

In 2020 alone, in response to the pandemic, countries either further opened up their markets or tightened their markets to protect local industry in different service areas. For example, some countries relaxed restrictions in the areas of telemedicine and telecommunication. France loosened restrictions on telemedicine services from March until May 31, 2020, for any individual affected by COVID-19 and other patients under certain circumstances, regardless of any existing or prior relationship between the healthcare provider and the patient. France allowed the use of internet platforms and other apps, as well as the use of telephones.

India also responded by relaxing some of its rules on telecommunications to allow for its use in various areas such as medicine, banking, education, and e-commerce. According to a March 2020 public announcement by the Indian Ministry of Communications, these revised rules were scheduled to take effect up to April 30, 2020.

When it came to the financial services sector, several countries tightened restrictions in response to COVID-19. The WTO published these measures in an effort to maintain transparency and without any determination. For example, Canada indicated that any foreign investments in Canadian businesses, especially those in the areas of public health or related to the provision of critical goods and services to Canadian citizens or the Canadian government, would face increased scrutiny under the Investment Canada Act. The Canadian government publicized this policy in April 2020 which would remain until the Canadian economy recovered from the impact created by the pandemic.

In April 2020, India also implemented greater restrictions on foreign investment. The new policy placed restrictions on company acquisition and added the requirement for government permission for any organization or citizen of a country that shares a border with India prior to investing in India.

GATS sets the framework under which service suppliers operate. The first part of understanding that framework is comprehending how services are defined in GATS.

Four Modes of Supply of Services

The key aspects of GATS are how services are supplied in the global economy. The four modes of supply in GATS (Article I:2)—cross border supply, consumption abroad, commercial presence, and presence of natural persons—distinguish ways in which services are provided internationally.

Mode 1: Cross-border Supply. The first mode of supply, cross border supply, refers to the supply of a service from the territory of one WTO member into the territory of another. Examples of cross-border supply include telecommunications, consulting services, telemedicine, and distance education.

Mode 2: Consumption Abroad. This mode refers to the services supplies in the territory of one WTO member to consumers from any other member territories. Students traveling abroad to consume educational services and medical patients receiving treatment in another country are examples of the consumption abroad mode.

Mode 3: Commercial Presence. Services provided under this mode of supply involve a service provider from one member territory setting up in another member territory through ownership or leasing on the premises in order to provide a service. One such example of commercial presence is the establishment of a hotel chain from one country in different parts of the world.

Mode 4: Presence of natural persons. This mode means that the service is provided by individuals from one country or territory who enter another country or territory to do so, as in the case of medical doctors. The people providing the services do not have to be a citizen, resident, or have permanent employment in the other country or territory.

Notably, all four modes can apply simultaneously. "For example, a foreign company established under mode 3 in country A may employ nationals from country B (mode 4) to export services cross-border into countries B, C, etc."

(WTO "GATS Training Module"). These modes of supply make it clear as to the types of services by any given business in the service sector that are covered under GATS.

GATS Commitments

Chapter 5 discussed the basic negotiation framework and final structure of trade deals at the bilateral, regional, and cross-regional levels. A similar framework can be found in GATS, in which members agree to binding commitments that would allow for the continued services trade across borders. Members agree to general obligations that apply to all members and services sectors. Specific commitments are negotiated commitments pertaining to a particular service sector. There are still specific commitments that are being negotiated in pursuant to Article XIX, which calls for the progressive liberalization of services through additional rounds of negotiations. This same article stipulates that a new round of negotiations begin no later than five years from the date that the WTO Agreement took effect, which was January 1, 1995. Negotiations began in 2000 and continued as part of the Doha Round of Negotiations that started a year later. The goal of these negotiations was to increase the levels of trade liberalization in services, while also taking into account national policy objectives and levels of economic development, and growing the level of commitment among members. The four top negotiation areas are market access, domestic regulation, GATS rules, and implementation of LDC modalities.

Market Access. GATS Article XVI says: "With respect to market access through the modes of supply…each Member shall accord services and service suppliers of any other Member treatment no less favourable than that provided for under the terms, limitations, and conditions agreed and specified in its Schedule." In other words, members agree to provide other members the same treatment and that which follows the terms set under the article.

Furthermore, the market access commitment under Article XVI:2 prohibits certain discriminatory and restrictive measures that hinder access to foreign service providers such as quantitative restrictions (e.g., quotas) on the number of foreign service suppliers, the total value of service transactions or assets, the total number of service operations or the total amount of service output, and the total number of natural persons that can be employed in a specific service sector or that a service provider can employ. Other measures that Article XVI:2 prohibits include restrictions on the type of legal entity or joint venture required for a service supplier to provide a service and limitations on the foreign capital.

Domestic Regulation. The members agree to not set local "qualification requirements and procedures, technical standards, and licensing requirements and procedures" that result in creating an unnecessary barrier to trade (GATS Article VI: 4).

GATS Rules. Three specific areas of emergency safeguard measures, government procurement, and subsidies are the focus of the GATS rules for which members still needed to discuss and finalize an agreement even after the conclusion of the Uruguay Round. The Hong Kong Ministerial Declaration resulted in Annex C, which required negotiators to boost their efforts to finalize negotiations regarding these specific areas. These negotiations are carried out by the Working Party on GATS Rules.

Safeguard measures go as far back as GATT Article XIX and refer to those actions taken by a government to temporarily restrict the import of a product in an effort to protect local producers from the potential or actual harm caused to the industry by an increase in imports. However, these safeguard measures allowed under GATT were sometimes used as a form of protectionism. Emergency safeguard measures (ESMs) became a part of talks surrounding trade in services. Article X of GATS emphasizes the use of safeguard measures, such as the suspension of concessions or obligations, as a way to address any harm or potential to cause injury to the domestic industry of any importing members. The first paragraph of the ESM Article reads, "There shall be multilateral negotiations on the question of emergency safeguard measures based on the principle of non-discrimination. The results of such negotiations shall enter into effect on a date not later than three years from the date of entry into force of the WTO Agreement" (WTO "General Agreement on Trade in Services").

The most recent information regarding that status of these talks is an April 2011 progress report published on the WTO website. According to the report, in 2009, the Working Party held more than a round of technical discussions regarding the definition of "domestic industry": how the "domestic industry" is treated under the WTO Agreements on anti-dumping, subsidies, and safeguards; and the relevance to trade in services. A year later, the technical discussions continued and some members pushed for a "presentation on the availability and adequacy of services statistics with respect to emergency safeguards."

Government procurement is another area of focus under the GATS rules, which was addressed under Article XIII. This particular article encouraged multilateral negotiations on government procurement in services, meaning that all members would participate in the negotiations. The emphasis on multilateralism advances the WTO Agreement on Government Procurement, which allows for talks among countries with similar interests rather than all WTO members. Article XIII calls for negotiations within two years of the WTO Agreement taking effect. According to the WTO:

> The lack of multilateral rules covering government procurement has been perceived as a significant gap in the international trading system. Government procurement represents between 15 and 20 per cent of GDP, and procurement of services constitutes a substantial part of this total. Likewise, access to government procurement markets and contracts, including foreign ones, is an important factor for the competitiveness of individual service suppliers. (WTO "Negotiations")

Additionally, Article XIII indicates that other articles pertaining to MFN treatment, market access, and national treatment do not "apply to laws, regulations or requirements governing the procurement by governmental agencies of services purchased for governmental purposes and not with a view to commercial resale or with a view to use in the supply of services for commercial sale." Unlike the bilateral, regional, and cross-regional agreements discussed in Chapter 5, multilateral binding rules on government procurement are lacking.

Article XV focuses on subsidies, which also fall under the GATS Rules category. This article calls for negotiations to create rules that serve to prevent the trade distortion caused by subsidies. At the same time, negotiations should take into account the need for some countries, especially developing countries, to use subsidies and require members to share information about any subsidies provided to domestic service suppliers and that are related to trade in services. Nevertheless, the obligations of MFN treatment (Article II) and national treatment (Article XVII) apply to the use of subsidies. In other words, discrimination against trading partners is prohibited and that subsidies offered to domestic suppliers must also be accessible by foreign service providers. These obligations continue to govern subsidy practices as an agreed-upon multilateral agreement has yet to be completed since the Doha Round of negotiations stalled.

Implementation of LDC modalities (Article IV: 3) offers special and differential treatment to LDCs. Before going into details about this article still under negotiation, it is important to note that the preamble to the GATS shows an emphasis on including developing countries in trade in services. The preamble reads:

> Recognizing the growing importance of trade in services for the growth and development of the world economy. Wishing to establish a multilateral framework of principles and rules for trade in services with a view to the expansion of such trade under conditions of transparency and progressive liberalization and as a means of promoting the economic growth of all trading partners and the development of developing countries. Desiring to facilitate the increasing participation of developing countries in trade in services and the expansion of their service exports including, *inter alia*, through the strengthening of their domestic services capacity and its efficiency and competitiveness. Taking particular account of the serious difficulty of the least-developed countries in view of their special economic situation and their development, trade and financial needs.

Article IV expands on the idea by requiring members to negotiate specific commitments that would allow developing countries to improve their domestic services capacity and provide special treatment to LDCs.

The GATS includes general obligations to the four negotiation areas listed below. For clarification purposes, some of those additional obligations include the following:

MFN Treatment - Article II (Part II - General Obligations and Disciplines)
Transparency - Article III (Part II - General Obligations and Disciplines)
National Treatment - Article XVII (Part III - Specific Commitments)
Dispute Settlement - Article XXIII (Part V - Institutional Provisions)

Article XXIV establishes the Council for Trade in Services, which "shall carry out such functions as may be assigned to it to facilitate the operation of this Agreement and further its objectives." The members select the Chairperson of the Council.

GATS Provisions by Sector

The GATS text includes several annexes that address specific types of services. The sector-based provisions include services in air transport, finance, maritime transport, and telecommunications.

Air transport. GATS, as well as the dispute settlement process, does not apply to traffic rights. Traffic rights refer to the rights granted to "scheduled and non-scheduled services to operate and/or carry passengers, cargo, and mail" for payment or hire within or over any member country or territory. However, GATS applies to measures that impact aircraft repair and maintenance services, selling and marketing of air transport services, and computer reservations system services.

Financial Services. The Annex on Financial Services mainly focused on several GATS measures affecting the supply of financial services. One area discussed in the annex is the application of the four modes of supply outlined in Article I.2 of the Agreement. The Annex also discusses the application of domestic regulation (Article VI) and recognition (Article VII). Dispute settlement procedures (Article XXIII) apply in the sense that panels for disputes on "prudential issues" must have necessary expertise pertinent to the specific financial service under dispute. The Annex applies to all members.

Maritime transport. Negotiations surrounding maritime transport were scheduled to conclude in June 1996, two years after the conclusion of the Uruguay Round of negotiations. The members could not reach an agreement on commitments in this area. The talks started again in 2000. In 2005, members presented their sectoral and modal objectives for the maritime transport negotiations (see World Trade Organization TN/S/23 November 2005). These are applied to three areas of maritime transport: international shipping, auxiliary services, and access to the use of port facilities.

Telecommunications. Similar to maritime transport, the annex on telecommunications focuses on the application of MFN treatment and any exemptions from Annex Article II toward this industry. Members must also report any measures that are inconsistent with MFN treatment.

GATS and Digital Trade

As Sections I and II have shown, e-commerce has grown in significance when it comes to cross-border trade. The importance is demonstrated both in terms of e-commerce service suppliers (e.g. Amazon, Alibaba) and service providers who use e-commerce to reach other markets (see Meltzer 2015 for more). This trend raises the question as to how GATS applies to e-commerce and other technologies, such as blockchain technology, that facilitate cross-border trade in services. Answers to this question will be provided in this section.

E-commerce is defined as the "advertising, sale, and distribution of products or services electronically" (WT/L/274 September 30, 1998). The definition includes digital items such as music, videos, apps, and games that are downloaded and paid for online. Additionally, service transactions online between the provider and end-user in two different countries are included.

The Work Programme on Electronic Commerce in 1998 set a framework for e-commerce. During this time, WTO members agreed to duty-free treatment for electronic transmissions.

During the Doha Round in 2002, the WTO members agreed to continue the practice of not placing customs duties on electronic transmissions. Two issues over which negotiations have not moved forward pertain to: 1) whether digital products should be classified as goods or services (Sauvé et al. 2006; Fleuter 2016) and 2) whether to extend the moratorium on customs duties on electronic transmissions (Banga 2020; IISD 2020). The classification would determine whether they could operate under GATT, which applies to all members, or GATS, which is flexible and allows only important obligations that apply if the member chooses to do so.

The WTO merely lays out a framework within which to govern e-commerce trade without directly regulating e-commerce trade. In other words, the WTO does not determine which sites users can surf, how to protect the privacy of users, or the price of the internet (Wunsch-Vincent n.d., xi). Four bodies within the WTO are responsible for implementing the Work Programme on Electronic Commerce. They are the Council for Trade in Services, the Council for Trade in Goods, the Council for TRIPS, and the Committee on Trade and Development. Ongoing review is conducted by the General Council.

The GATS Modes 1 and 2 mainly apply to e-commerce, because of the activity of both cross-border supply and consumption abroad. Furthermore, electronic delivery of services is based on Article I of GATS, which describes the different modes of supply of services.

Article III on transparency applies to the electronic supply of a service. Article VI applies to prevent any practices or domestic regulations that become unnecessary barriers to trade while also applying XIV (General Exceptions) for privacy protection and fraud prevention while not resulting in barriers to trade and discriminatory trade practices. Market access and national treatment also apply. As the case study in this chapter will show, the lack of clear, set rules for e-commerce has created a problem for business owners and the WTO.

The book has discussed other technologies such as blockchain, which also allows for the provision of services. Two more questions emerge. What does GATS say about services that rely on blockchain or other digital technologies, if anything at all? If these other technologies are addressed, how does GATS apply to digital technology beyond e-commerce?

The multilateral services framework does not directly incorporate blockchain into its commitments and obligations. As one would expect, the *Services Sectoral Classification List* produced during the Uruguay Round in 1991, which refers to the 1991 United Nations Provisional Central Product Classification (CPC) (see section IV), did not include blockchain. However, the Services Sectoral Classification List includes computer services and related services as a sub-sector under the business services sector. The specific computer and related services include the following:

- Consultancy services related to the installation of computer hardware
- Software implementation services
- Data processing services
- Database services
- Other

The 2015 CPC version 2.1 expands on the services within the overall information technology industry (IT), with an emphasis on consulting and support services (8313). The different services-based sub-classes for IT in this newer version include:

- IT consulting services
- IT support services
- IT design and development services
- IT design and development services for applications
- IT design and development services for networks and systems
- Software originals
- Hosting and informational technology (IT) infrastructure provisioning services
- Website hosting services
- Application service provisioning
- Other hosting and IT infrastructure provisioning services (include, *inter alia*, "data management services, i.e., on-going management and administration of data as an organizational resource. (Services may include

performing data modeling, data mobilization, data mapping/rationalization, data mining and system architecture.")

■ IT infrastructure and networking management services
■ Network management services
■ Computer systems management services
■ Other management services, except construction project management services

The updated version of the CPC has the potential to serve as a guide for WTO members when addressing digital trade, especially with regard to blockchain technology (see Razon 2019, 135).

Whereas the WTO has yet to resolve this matter by engaging in negotiations and setting specific commitments and obligations, the debate within the international trade law community continues regarding whether these technologies should fall under GATT or GATS or an interpretation as to how GATS is the most appropriate framework for understanding and enforcing policies regarding digital trade. For instance, in Chapter 8 on e-commerce and digital technologies, one suggestion was to make sure that one is aware of the national-level policies regarding cryptocurrency, specifically, since there is not a single international-level standard. Some have argued that these domestic laws that prohibit cryptocurrencies and other blockchain apps or services violate the measures under GATS. "Such measures, in so far as they constitute barriers to international trade in services and violate existing commitments of a member, may be challenged before WTO's dispute settlement system, dubbed the 'bedrock of the multilateral trading system' and 'the jewel in the crown of the WTO'" (Razon 2019, pp. 137).

Other areas that are left, as has taken place with the importance of e-commerce alone, are to determine the mode of supply that applies to blockchain, classification of the type of service, and, based on that, the GATS measures that would apply to blockchain both when it comes to the obligations and specific sectoral commitments.

Observations and Analysis

International trade in services, especially in the area of digital trade, is far more complex than trade in goods, for which there is a tangible product with a harmonized code to determine preferential access. Services can include non-tangible products and focus on regulatory barriers that can restrict trade in services. With digital trade things become more complex as questions such as classification alone arise to address the technologies that have emerged and play a significant role in cross-border trade since the original measures set forth in the Uruguay Round and stalled Doha Round of negotiations.

Another area of focus, not mentioned above, relates to the GATS emphasis on developing economies and LDCs. That has been a debate as to how these measures, such as the moratorium on customs duties on electronic transmissions, affect developing countries. Without a strong framework that directly addresses these new technologies, digital trade is still open to interpretation.

This book focuses on the linkages between business practices and policies. The previous chapter showed how domestic politics can spill over into the multilateral negotiation space and affect negotiation outcomes or stall any progress altogether. With varying levels of interest regarding digital trade, this would be just one more such matter. Until this hurdle can be overcome, what is suggested in the following paragraph for the benefit of the international trade regime and the service suppliers that operate within it may be just a stated idea for now.

It may seem like a lot of legalese when it comes to understanding the rules, commitments, etc., regarding international trade in services. Nevertheless, it is these rules put forth by government negotiators by which it is important to understand the implications for and how they are applied to companies from different industries within the larger services sector, as in the case study presented here. In other words, the case below shows how international trade policy toward services, domestic policies, and business practices collide.

Case Study 10.1 US-Antigua Gambling Services Case

The U.S.-Antigua Gambling Services Case brought the issue of internet services and how it is governed under GATS to the forefront when Jay Cohen, CEO of World Sports Exchange, was the first U.S. citizen convicted of violating the U.S. Wire Act. World Sports Exchange was an online gaming company based in Antigua and Barbuda that existed from 1995 to 2012. In 1998, Mr. Cohen; his business partners, Steve Schillinger and Hayden Ware; and 17 other U.S. citizens from other online gaming companies were accused of violating the U.S. Wire Act. The U.S. Wire Act is a 1961 federal law that banned telephones or wire communications to make bets. Mr. Cohen returned to the United States to fight the charge but was found guilty in 2000 and sentenced to 21 months in prison and fined US$5,000, making him the first person convicted under the U.S. Wire Act as a result of his cross-border gambling services. Manhattan U.S. Attorney Mary Jo White said about the case:

> An Internet communication is no different than a telephone call for purpose of liability under the Wire Wager Act. As this case demonstrates, persons convicted of operating Internet sportsbooks offshore face very serious consequences—imprisonment and thousands of dollars in fines.

(Reuters 2000)

However, this was not the end of the case. In *U.S. v Cohen (2001)*, Cohen's defense team argued that the conviction violated GATS. The case extended beyond that of a businessperson to the government of Antigua filing a dispute settlement case in March 2003, in which it argued that the restriction against online gambling services in Antigua that reached U.S. consumers violated the GATS principles. The case became known as the U.S.-Measures Affecting the Cross-Border Supply of Gambling and Betting Services (DS285). Here are the key arguments and the measures and corresponding articles that were applied in this case for both Antigua and the United States:

Antigua

Market Access (Article XVI). Antigua argued that the U.S. Wire Act, as well as the Travel Act (1961), and the Illegal Gambling Business Act (IGBA) (1970) violated the specific commitment under Market Access by discriminating against foreign gambling and betting services, including providers from Antigua, while allowing U.S. services to continue to operate (Jackson 2012, 377). The original dispute settlement panel and the Appellate Body found that these U.S. laws were in violation of XVI: 1 and 2 of GATS.

Other Recreational Services (Except for Sporting) (Sub-sector 10.D). Antigua argued further that the U.S. laws were in violation of the GATS Sub-sector 10.D which calls for free trade for recreational services, except for sporting. The panel ruled that online gambling and betting services did not fall under sporting, and the U.S. laws violated the commitments that it made under Sub-sector 10.D.

United States

General Exceptions (Article XIV). The United States argued that its laws did not violate GATS rules, because Article XIV allows for discriminatory practices to protect public morals. Article XIV reads as follows:

> Subject to the requirement that such measures are not applied in a manner which would constitute a means of arbitrary or unjustifiable discrimination between countries where like conditions prevail, or a disguised restriction on trade in services, nothing in this Agreement shall be construed to prevent the adoption or enforcement by any Member of measures: (a) necessary to protect public morals or to maintain public order…The public order exception may be invoked only where a genuine and sufficiently serious threat is posed to one of the fundamental interests of society. (WTO "General Agreement on Trade in Services")

The dispute settlement panel did not find the U.S. argument on the basis of protecting public morals convincing. As a result, the panel ruled that the discriminatory practices on the part of the United States do not fall under the guidelines set forth by GATS Article XIV. In other words, the United States was unsuccessful in demonstrating that its prohibition of online gambling services from foreign suppliers, such as Antigua, were "necessary" to protect citizens on moral grounds (WT/DS285/R November 10 2004 ruling and WT/DS285/RW Opening Statement by the United States November 27, 2006, Executive Summary Annex D-2).

Overall, the dispute settlement panel ruled that the U.S. laws were designed to restrict trade in services, specifically with regard to online gambling and betting services. Antigua was awarded the ability to suspend its obligations under the Trade Related Intellectual Property (TRIPS) under GATS Articles XXI–XXII in retaliation to make up for the damages. However, over 10 years after the final ruling by the Appellate Body in 2007, the United States has not complied with the Dispute Settlement Body (DSB) ruling, which leads to questions about the effectiveness of the enforcement mechanism for the producers, industries, and economies affected (see Lumsden 2018 for more).

Bibliography

Banga, Rashmi. 2020. "Should digitally delivered products be exempted from customs duties?" In United Nations Conference on Trade and Development.

Fleuter, Sam. 2016. "The role of digital products under the WTO: A new framework for GATT and GATS classification." *Chicago Journal of International Law* 17 (1):153–177.

IISD (International Institute for Sustainable Development). 2020. WTO Members Highlight Benefits and Drawbacks of E-commerce Moratorium. International Institute for Sustainable Development.

Jackson, Sarita D. 2012. "Small states and compliance bargaining in the WTO: An analysis of the Antigua –US Gambling Services Case." *Cambridge Review of International Affairs* 25 (3):367–385.

Lumsden, Andrew. 2018. *Blowing the Dice: Hurricane Sends Decade-Old U.S.-Antigua Dispute Back into the Spotlight.* Washington, DC: Council on Hemispheric Affairs.

Razon, Arvin Kristopher. 2019. "Liberalising Blockchain: An Application of the GATS Digital Trade Framework." *Melbourne Journal of International Law* Vol. 20: 125–57.

Reuters. 2000. "Man jailed in 1st U.S. online gambling conviction." *New York Times*, August 11.

Sauvé, Pierre. 2006. "An introduction to global subsidies." *Global Subsidies Initiative.* Accessed September 30, 2020. https://www.iisd.org/gsi/commentary/introduction-service-subsidies.

WTO (World Trade Organization). n.d.a. "GATS training module: Chapter 1." Accessed September 30, 2020. https://www.wto.org/english/tratop_e/serv_e/cbt_course_e/c1s3p1_e.htm.

WTO. n.d.b. "General agreement on trade in services." Accessed September 30, 2020. https://www.wto.org/english/tratop_e/serv_e/gatsintr_e.htm.

WTO. n.d.c. "General agreement on trade in services (GATS): Objectives, coverage, and disciplines." Accessed September 30, 2020. https://www.wto.org/english/tratop_e/serv_e/gatsqa_e.htm#.

WTO. n.d.d. "Negotiations on GATS rules." Accessed September 30, 2020. https://www.wto.org/english/tratop_e/serv_e/gats_rules_negs_e.htm.

Wunsch-Vincent, Sacha. n.d. "WTO, E-commerce, and information technologies from the Uruguay round through the Doha development agenda." Accessed September 30, 2020. https://www.piie.com/publications/papers/wunsch1104.pdf.

Chapter 11

Trade in Services Agreement

It has been labeled the "most important free trade agreement you've never heard of." It has even been controversial following critics' concerns surrounding what they considered a secretive negotiation process, among other things. However, finding the mention of, or an in-depth review of, this proposed agreement in textbooks or during workshops for business students and business owners becomes similar to looking for a needle in a haystack. The referenced proposed agreement is the Trade in Services Agreement (TiSA).

TiSA was an agreement that was under negotiation from 2013 to 2016 in response to the lack of progress with GATS during the WTO Doha Round, as discussed in Chapter 9. The 23 negotiating parties sought to enhance the liberalization of trade in services. Those parties include the following: Australia, Canada, Chile, Colombia, Costa Rica, European Union (28), Hong Kong, Iceland, Israel, Japan, Liechtenstein, Mauritius, Mexico, New Zealand, Norway, Pakistan, Panama, Peru, South Korea, Switzerland, Taiwan, Turkey, and the United States.* At the time, the United States did not state a clear position on TISA. However, in the summer of 2017, U.S. Trade Representative Robert Lighthizer mentioned to lawmakers that TiSA was an important deal (ICTSD 2017). The talks eventually stalled in November 2016. Although TISA has stalled, this chapter just provides a simple and brief overview of the significance of the agreement had it been signed and taken effect.

TiSA differed from GATS in a couple of ways. The first distinction rests with the plurilateral approach under TiSA compared to GATS. A plurilateral agreement means that there would be a limited number of signatories.

---

* Uruguay and Paraguay withdrew from the negotiations in 2015.

Oftentimes, a plurilateral deal covers a specific sector or industry rather than being comprehensive. Only the signatories to the agreement enjoy the benefits of the final agreement.

It is worth noting that the flexibility of GATS also allows for some plurilateral provisions. GATS "shall not prevent any of its Members from being a party to or entering into an agreement liberalizing trade in services between or among the parties to such an agreement, provided that such an agreement … has substantial coverage" (GATS Article V). The U.S.-based shipping service company, UPS, has publicly pushed for a plurilateral initiative using GATS to eliminate gender discrimination against women in international trade. In a May 2020 piece that appeared on the UPS website titled, "Women in Trade Can Reinvigorate the Global Economy," Lane and Naas write:

> Members can support the ability of women to participate in international trade by making a horizontal commitment in their General Agreement on Trade in Services (GATS) schedules, stating that none of the GATS commitments that countries have made will discriminate against individuals based on gender….To that end, the WTO has a number of flexible and non-traditional negotiating tools at hand…Another approach is a WTO plurilateral agreement on women in trade, through which willing WTO members could come together to codify the elimination of discrimination against women in trade. Such an agreement would eliminate domestic laws that perpetuate such discrimination and ensure compliance with the principles of equal access and opportunity for trade.

The other difference between TiSA and GATS is that the former would have been separate from the WTO. Willing parties to TiSA would operate under the negotiated terms of the agreement, which would be separate from the WTO altogether. Notably, the European Commission fact-sheet states, "For the EU, TiSA is intended to be a forerunner of a multilateral agreement on services that would be folded into the WTO once critical mass is reached."

The TISA parties represented 70% of the world's trade in services of the $55 trillion services market worldwide. According to the USTR in 2016, the agreement is important because it would level the playing field for U.S. service supplies globally. In other words, TISA would restrict policies and practices favoring domestic service suppliers over foreign suppliers, thereby limiting competition. Furthermore, the USTR argued in favor of TISA, because it would allow U.S. service suppliers, who provide services from telecommunications to delivery services, to enjoy the same access to foreign markets that many overseas suppliers enjoy in the U.S. market.

TiSA will still build from the obligation and commitment within GATS while enhancing the commitments in the service-specific chapters. Based on the information that has been made public about TiSA, the agreement would have been organized into four areas:

1. Build upon GATS and include horizontal provisions that would be applicable all across the agreement,
2. Establish the commitments as they pertain to market access and national treatment, including member schedules and any exceptions,
3. Sectoral regulatory annexes,
4. Institutional provisions regarding the function of the agreement (Fefer 2017).

The European Commission published a 2016 fact sheet breaking down the key rules, both horizontal provisions and sector-based rules, that were being negotiated. The rules that were being negotiated include the following:

■ Transparency—obligations regarding how current laws and regulations will be made available to the public
■ Domestic regulations—develop a system to streamline the rules and regulations pertaining to licensing and authorization to supply a service, while also ensuring fairness and transparency
■ Localization—requirements for foreign service suppliers in areas requiring the purchase of domestically supplied services, providing a service using a local facility, the transfer of technology or intellectual property, or compliance with country-specific standards
■ Movement of natural persons (Mode 4)—rules regarding the movement of highly skilled professionals from one country to another

Sectoral Annexes

■ E-commerce—rules pertaining to all types of trade that occurs via electronic means and digital trade
■ Financial services—rules for all financial services, which include banking, insurance, and insurance-related services, to facilitate trade in this area

■ Transport: Maritime, Air, and Road services—provisions to increase market access in this area
■ Delivery services—also to further liberalize trade in the area of delivery services—refers to the collection, sorting, movement, and delivery of documents, goods, etc. by a commercial delivery operator (public or private)

A list of items that are not covered under TiSA include:

■ Public services
■ Audiovisual services
■ Investment protection/Investor-to-state dispute settlement
■ Data protection

According to the same European Commission report, 17 negotiating texts were a part of the talks, although it was unclear at that time which of these actual texts or annexes would make it to the final agreement.

Proponents of TiSA believed that it would further liberalize trade in services. For instance, the European Commission has put forth the idea that TiSA would lower service trade costs by 3.4% in OECD countries and 5.8% in low- and middle-income countries. A U.S. Congressional Research Service study highlights the benefits of TiSA as leveling the playing field and providing new market opportunities for service suppliers (Fefer 2017).

Opponents, on the other hand, highlighted a wide range of issues starting with transparency. Wikileaks published documents from the negotiations and argued that the TiSA talks lacked transparency. The European Commission goes further to address the matter of transparency in the following statement also published on its website, "Like any other trade negotiation, the TiSA talks are not carried out in public and the documents are available to participants only." Nevertheless, reports from the rounds of negotiations from 2013 to 2016 can be found on the European Commission website.

Another area of concern among critics includes the powerful influence of corporate lobbyists (Public Services International 2016). Some have argued that TiSA would threaten banks and state-owned enterprises (Public Services International 2017, Barreto and Chavez 2017, Marois 2017). With regard to e-commerce, concerns about privacy protection have also been raised (see Fefer 2017).

In sum, the TiSA would have provided another framework for international trade in services. Although the talks stalled in 2016 and were not free of controversy, TiSA is still worth following should there be any kind of turning point to restore the talks. Also, the agreement is worth following should it set the stage for any future efforts to move the rules in trade in services beyond that of the Doha Round.

Bibliography

Barreto, Viviana; and Daniel Chavez. 2017. *TiSA and state-owned enterprises: Lessons from Uruguay's withdrawal for other countries in the South.* Transnational Institute and REDES. Accessed September 30, 2020. https://www.tni.org/en/publication/tisa-and-state-owned-enterprises.

European Commission. 2016. *Trade in Services Agreement (Tisa) Factsheet.* Brussels, Belgium: European Commission.

Fefer, Rachel F. 2017. *Trade in Services Agreement (Tisa) Negotiations: Overview and Issues for Congress.* Washington, D.C.: Congressional Research Service.

ICTSD (International Centre for Trade and Sustainable Development). 2017. *Lighthizer Lays Out US Trade Policy Agenda, NAFTA Hearings Get Underway.* BRIDGES. Accessed October 2, 2020. https://ictsd.iisd.org/bridges-news/bridges/news/lighthizer-lays-out-us-trade-policy-agenda-nafta-hearings-get-underway.

Lane, Laura; and Penny Naas. 2020. *Women in Trade Can Reinvigorate the WTO and Global Economy.* UPS. Accessed September 30, 2020. https://www.ups.com/us/es/services/knowledge-center/article.page?name=women-in-trade-can-reinvigorate-the-wto-and-global-economy&kid=art17208e49584.

Marois, Thomas. 2017. *TiSA and the Threat to Public Banks.* Amsterdam: Transnational Institute. Accessed September 30, 2020. https://www.tni.org/en/publication/tisa-and-the-threat-to-public-banks.

Public Service International. 2016. Report shows corporate lobbyists dominate Tisa talks.

Public Services International. 2017. New reports warn of TiSA threat to public banks and SOEs.

Chapter 12

Conclusion

As this book has shown, trade in services has always been a significant part of international trade. The cross-border trade in services continues to grow and evolve. Hopefully, the information shared in this book will lead to more discussions about trade in services at the practical and policy levels. Until then, the insights and lessons shared here should be a good starting point for those business owners and executives who are interested in exporting a service to a foreign market.

One theme that emerged from the conversations with service suppliers is that building and nurturing long-term relationships with individuals who can serve as a resource or a collaborator is key. Furthermore, developing a strong network with individuals in various foreign markets helps one to know how to approach opportunities in those markets.

Research on a market, as it applies to a specific service, is still a must, especially with designing a sustainable strategy. The book highlights the key ingredients of a customized market design to improve a service provider's chance for international success.

Additionally, understanding the context within which one may work in a foreign market remains crucial, as several of the interviewees mentioned. One relevant theme related to the idea of moving away from one's own ideas and methods to solve problems in another country. Rather, it is important to forge local partnerships and understand the system politically, economically, and socially. Also, identifying a need in a market is just the first step to leveraging an opportunity. The next step is to know how that service should be provided to the end user.

Policies are established to allow service suppliers to gain greater and easier access to an overseas market. These policies impact a service supplier's ability to compete. While they do set a framework under which service suppliers operate, the policies leave much to be desired in terms of keeping up with technological advances. With the continuously growing digital economy, many trade agreements, including the General Agreement on Trade in Services (GATS), lack clear-cut rules and enforcement mechanisms to liberalize digital trade while also ensuring privacy protections and addressing cybersecurity matters. The US–Mexico–Canada Agreement (USMCA) modernized the North American Free Trade Agreement by considering the current digital economy. The USMCA took effect in 2020 and may set the precedent for future trade talks and agreements when it comes to digital trade.

Index

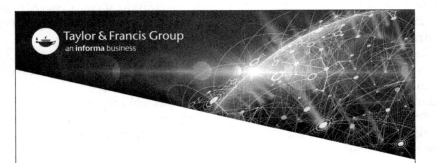

Printed in the United States
By Bookmasters